Cromer Lif

A pictorial history

Nicholas Leach and Paul Russell

Dedicated to Henry 'Shrimp' Davies, BEM, Coxswain of the Cromer Lifeboat from 1947 to 1976, and all who have served the Cromer lifeboat station since 1804.

Published by
Landmark Publishing Ltd
Ashbourne Hall
Cokayne Avenue
Ashbourne
Derbyshire DE6 1EJ
England
Tel (01335) 347349 Fax (01335) 347303
landmark@clara.net
www.landmarkpublishing.co.uk

ISBN 9781843063636

British Library Cataloguing in Publication Data: a catalogue record for this book is available from the British Library.

Book design and layout by Nicholas Leach
Cover design by Sarah Labuhn
Printed by Gutenberg Press, Malta

Cover photo: 16m Tamar *Lester* is launched down the slipway for the first time. (Nicholas Leach)

Frontispiece: *Lester* is put through her paces off Cromer pier, January 2008. (Nicholas Leach)

Back cover upper: Memorial to Coxswain Henry Blogg on the East Cliff. (Nicholas Leach)

Back cover lower: The Watson class lifeboat *Henry Blogg*, which served at Cromer from 1945 to 1967.

Cromer Lifeboats

A pictorial history

Contents

Subscribers

B. Aldis, Cromer
S. J. Aldridge, Belper
D. Allen, Canada
M. Arnold OBE, Overstrand
M. L. Ayden, Downham Market
I. Baker, Pelsall
E. Barnes, Draycott
S. A. Besley, Roughton
D. J. Billington, Cromer
C. Bowley, Tunbridge Wells
L. V. Bray, Cromer
F. & S. Brittain, Aylmerton
P. Britton, Cromer
M. & D. Broughton, Cromer
I. Chambers, Cromer
C. Chandler, Petersfield
K. J. Cheeseman, Cromer
J. Clipstone, Burton Latimer
M. Coates, Derby
C. Crone, Jedburgh
E. A. Dack, Cromer
M. A. Davis, Cromer
Dr R. Dawson, Avening
Mrs Downs, North Harrow
S. Dudley, Cromer
A. R. Eales, Cromer
F. J. Eastell, Cromer
D. G. Edwards, Cromer
R. Ely, Cromer
S. Evans, Leominster
D. M. & K. G. Ewles, North Walsham
S. J. Fairclough, Edgware
C. Fancourt, Cromer
R. J. Ford, Walthamstow
C. A. Gartrell, Deepcut
S. P. Gleeson, Folkestone
S. J. Goldfinch, Tonbridge
N. J. Goodenough, Norwich
J. Goodenough, Norwich
Mrs Goodwin, Burton on Trent
A. S. Gowan, Cromer
K. Gower, Dagnall
B. Grace, Selby
A. J. Hearn, North Petherton
M. Hill, Cromer
M. F. Holliday, Trowell
A. J. Inkley, Spalding
M. V. Johnson, Cromer
C. C. Keay, Cromer
S. H. Laker, Billericay
J. Lane, Sheringham
M. Lawrie, Cromer
Dr A. Lennox, Cromer
T. Mallett, Hethersett
B. M. P. McDonald, Thurmaston
M. C. Morris, Rhyl
M. Munn, Dagnall
F. Murihead, Cromer
R. Neill, Braintree
I. Nicholls, Barwell
K. A. Olley, Cromer
S. M. Orton, Cromer
K. J. Penning, Cromer
P. C. Pike, Cromer
N. Ray, Cork
W. H. Reynolds, Petts Wood
A. Richards , Shapinsay
J. Sanders, Worcester
Mrs Shinn, Banningham
H. Sleath, Cromer
D. G. Stannard, Eccles-on-Sea
D. Strapps, Coventry
A. F. W. Thatcher, Olney
J. Truran, Chorley
M. Uddin, Cromer
V. Ward, Rowghton
M. J. Webber, Colchester
E. Williams, Cromer
Y. P. Williams, Cromer
L. M . Willins, Cromer
A. L. Wiseman, Cromer

Introduction

Cromer lifeboat station is one of the most famous of all the lifeboat stations operated by the Royal National Lifeboat Institution. For two centuries, the town's lifeboats have been ready to go to the aid of ships and people in distress off the north Norfolk coast and during the twentieth century its volunteer lifeboat crews gained a record of gallantry second to none when, led by the famous Coxswain Henry Blogg, they were involved in some of the most dramatic and courageous rescues ever undertaken.

Cromer is a town whose lifeboat is one of its most famous elements. The importance of the lifeboat to the town is amply demonstrated by the fact that the town is littered with lifeboat-related features. As well as artefacts, much has been written about the lifeboats and lifeboat men of Cromer, several books about the station have been produced, and indeed hundreds of photographs and postcards have been published showing the town's lifeboats. This book, however, is the first to tell the history of the station through photographs. The majority of the images reproduced in this volume have never been published before.

Inevitably the early years of the station are harder to document through illustrations than the later years, and so the book has a greater emphasis on events during those years from which photographs are most easily available. But Cromer is fortunate to have enjoyed the patronage of some talented photographers in an age when, unlike today, photography was a specialism pursued by very few. As a result, the town's lifeboats and lifeboat crews, as well as many rescues, have been unusually well documented in images.

Amongst the photographers who captured the history of the lifeboats and crews are David Savin, one of the early commercial photographers in the town, and Daniel Davison, who ran a pharmacy in Jetty Street and took photos in the late nineteenth and early twentieth centuries. In the early part of the twentieth century, A. J. Rogers had a studio in Church Street. He was succeeded by Harry Tansley between the

An unremarkable photo of *Harriot Dixon* on her carriage, but notable because the small boy watching events is author Paul Russell, now a resident of the town.

wars. Tansley took photos up to the 1950s, and was the only photographer operating in the town during the war. Many of his images of the Cromer lifeboats have been used widely in many publications.

The other notable photographer in the town was Philip Vicary, who had a passion for maritime photography and built up a successful business. Following on from Tansley and Vicary, photographers from the *Eastern Daily Press*, particularly Norman Taylor, took up the mantle of documenting the town's lifeboat happenings. Today, that newspaper, together with the *North Norfolk News*, keep the spotlight on events at the station at a time when news reporting and photography have entered the digital age.

As well as having some pioneering photographers, Cromer became a station at the forefront of developments and innovations in life-saving equipment, particularly when motor lifeboats made the station a key one along the east coast. The construction of the lifeboat house and slipway at the end of the pier in 1923 improved the launch procedure considerably. With its motor lifeboat and slipway launch, Cromer was uniquely placed on the east coast for a fast launch using the largest lifeboats available, which could not be manhandled on the sandy beaches common at most other places along the same coast.

The new boathouse also, coincidentally, gave photographers a new vantage point from which to capture lifeboats in action. The dramatic sight of the lifeboat entering the water during a slipway launch was an outstanding photographic subject. In fact, the splash of a lifeboat as it hits the water during a slipway launch is an iconic image of sea rescue in the British Isles. The new 16m Tamar maintains the tradition of slipway launching.

Several other notable milestones can be attributed to Cromer. The Cromer crew was the first to be awarded Bronze medals (in 1917) which were created specifically for a rescue they had performed. They were also the first to operate a motor lifeboat with midship steering and VHF radio (the 46ft Watson motor *Henry Blogg*). Recent lifeboats were early examples of their type with the 48ft 6in Oakley only the third of its type to be built, the Tyne the sixth of its class, and the Tamar only the fifth to go on station.

The new boathouse, the first to be built with the Tamar in mind, again pushed Cromer to the forefront of lifeboat development as the RNLI fulfils its aim of providing twenty-five-knot lifeboats at slipway stations. The town also boasts an impressive new lifeboat museum, which was built with the involvement of the RNLI's Heritage Trust and focuses on the station's history as well as its most famous figure, Coxswain Henry Blogg.

A well known photograph showing *H. F. Bailey* (ON.694) launching on lifeboat day, 15 August 1934, with the No.2 lifeboat *Harriot Dixon* in the background. (From an old postcard supplied by Paul Russell).

Cromer's 16m Tamar lifeboat *Lester* on her cradle in the lifeboat house ready for the next launch. (Nicholas Leach)

Martin Steward, Ady Barker, Paul Watling, Mearl Brown, John Davies and Ady Woods on board the 16m Tamar *Lester* at The Lifeboat College, Poole, 8 October 2007, while training on the new craft. (Nicholas Leach)

This book has been produced to coincide with the stationing of the new 16m Tamar lifeboat at Cromer, an advanced new craft which will give the crew the very best tool with which to continue the work of saving life at sea. It is also a tribute to the courage and bravery of the volunteer lifeboat crews of the RNLI.

Acknowledgements

The photographs in this book have come from a variety of sources, and the following have been particularly helpful in supplying images for possible inclusion: Donny Abbs, Ted Luckin, Joyce Blyth, Willie Cox, Peter Stibbons, Richard Leeds, Ros Davies, P. Poulter, David Leeder, Tony Rogers, David Gooch, Peter Edey, and Roger Wiltshire. Successive coxswains and crews, notably Richard and John Davies, have also helped in providing photograph opportunities, and we are grateful to them all. Thanks also to the staff at the *North Norfolk News* office in Cromer, and to Jenny Sheldrake from Archant in Norwich. Every effort has been made to correctly credit images, and we apologise if any are wrongly attributed; it is not known who took some of the photos. Finally, thanks to Chris Gilbert, at Landmark Publishing, for his patience throughout the preparation and production of this book; and to Sarah in Birmingham and Sarah in Cromer for their help and support.

Nicholas Leach and Paul Russell, January 2008

1804-1902 • The first lifeboats

Cromer's first lifeboat was built by Henry Greathead, of South Shields, in 1804. The double-ended boat, which was probably 25ft long by 8ft 6in in beam, had a rockered keel and would have been well-suited to drive through the surf off the beach. The boat was paid for through a subscription fund which was administered by a local committee led by Lord Suffield, the third baron of Gunton Park; George Wyndham of Cromer Hall; Thomas Mickleburgh, a local merchant; Joseph Gurney; and Benjamin Rust, a Cromer draper and grocer. She was delivered to the town early in 1805; an entry in the *Newcastle Courant* dated 6 April 1805 stated that 'Lifeboats had lately been sent by the inventor [Greathead] to the stations at Cromer and Leith.'

She was used for at least five rescues before being transferred to Wells in 1830 when the Norfolk Association had a second lifeboat built for the station. Like her predecessor, she remained unnamed and was kept on the beach. Her design closely resembled that of the first Greathead lifeboat as local builders around the river Tyne had copied Greathead's basic design lifeboat since the early nineteenth century. Reported to have cost £160, she was completed by Robson of Shields, was 31ft in length and rowed by twelve oars. This lifeboat was involved in at least four rescues, but by the 1850s, financial troubles made it increasingly difficult for the Norfolk Association to execute its duties. Its lifeboats had fallen into disrepair and it seems that, at Cromer, even organising a crew had become a problem. So, in December 1857, the Royal National Lifeboat Institution (RNLI) took over all of the Norfolk Association's stations.

During the second half of the nineteenth century, the RNLI implemented a series of improvements at Cromer, as well as at other lifeboat stations throughout the country, starting with the provision of a new 34ft twelve-oared self-righting lifeboat which arrived at the station in October 1858. This unnamed lifeboat remained until August 1868, when it was replaced by the first of two lifeboats named *Benjamin Bond Cabbell*, christened after the donor, of Cromer Hall, who, in November 1867, had agreed to provide for 'the whole expense of renovating the station.' The first of these two lifeboats was a standard self-righter, 34ft in length, pulling ten oars double-banked. The second, on station from September 1884 until 1902, was built to a non-self-righting design specifically for Cromer, and was 35ft in length with a beam of 10ft 6in. Although this unusual design was well liked at Cromer, only two other similar boats were built, both of which served in North Norfolk, operating from Wells and Blakeney.

This drawing, entitled 'A Perspective View of Mr H. Greathead's Life Boat going out to assist a Ship in Distress', dated 1802, was produced using a model presented by Greathead to the Admiralty and shows a boat similar to the first lifeboat used at Cromer.

A model of Cromer's first lifeboat, showing the ten oars and rockered keel. She was delivered to the station early in 1805, having been either towed to the station or delivered as deck cargo on one of the many colliers using the busy east coast trade route. By summer 1805, the boat was operational and, on 20 July 1805, a meeting of the subscribers was held at the New Inn to discuss the state of the fund and regulations for the future management of the boat. This model is now on display in the Henry Blogg Museum. (Poppyland)

The second Cromer lifeboat, on station from 1830 to 1858, is credited with saving at least fifteen lives and performed at least four rescues. She was similar in form to the first lifeboat and was based on the Greathead design but was slightly larger and pulled twelve oars double banked. She was funded through the efforts of the Norfolk Shipwreck Association, which was founded in November 1823 and managed the lifeboats at Cromer and Mundesley, as well as establishing stations elsewhere in Norfolk.

The brigantine *Agenoria*, of Lowestoft, wrecked opposite Cromer gangway on 9 April 1868. The first RNLI lifeboat saved the vessel's crew of five. The lifeboat is in the foreground with its carriage to the left.

Following problems with financing and managing its lifeboats, the Norfolk Association began negotiations with the RNLI which resulted in the Association's lifeboats and stations being taken over with effect from 29 December 1857. The RNLI immediately supplied a new lifeboat, a 34ft self-righter, which served for ten years before being replaced by this lifeboat, named *Benjamin Bond Cabbell*, pictured on her carriage on the East Beach. Built in 1868, she was a standard self-righting lifeboat, 34ft in length, pulling ten oars.

Recovery of the second *Benjamin Bond Cabbell* on the east beach. This photograph shows the effort required to haul the boat, with its rudder retracted, clear of the water prior to being recarriaged. Launching across the open beach could often be a difficult and physically demanding operation. (By courtesy of Gregory Vlamis)

The 1868-built *Benjamin Bond Cabbell* lifeboat on the beach. She was funded from the legacy of Benjamin Bond Cabbell, of Cromer Hall, who, in November 1867, had agreed to provide for 'the whole expense of renovating the station'. She served until 1884, launched on service nine times and saved thirty-one lives.

The schooner *Alpha* wrecked at East Runton in October 1883. Despite the lifeboat crew attempting to go to the schooner's aid, after the lifeboat launched she could make no headway, and as a result of the crew complaining about the inadequacy of the first *Benjamin Bond Cabbell*, a new lifeboat was sent to the station.

The second *Benjamin Bond Cabbell* lifeboat, which served from 1884 until 1902. This non-self-righting lifeboat was classified as a 'Cromer' type. Constructed by Beeching of Great Yarmouth, she was 35ft in length with a breadth of 10ft 6in, pulled fourteen oars, double-banked, and was fitted with a dipping lug sail.

The ketch *Hero*, of Goole, stranded on the rocks to the north of the jetty on 3 December 1897. Her crew of four were saved by the second *Benjamin Bond Cabbell.*

Launch of the second *Benjamin Bond Cabbell* from the east beach. The general lines of the Cromer type lifeboat, notably its raked stem and curved keel, are evident in this photograph. The type was also, at 10ft in beam, wider than the self-righting type lifeboat it replaced and would not right in the event of a capsize. With a good degree of manoeuvrability, it was fitted with water ballast tanks, had ten relieving valves and the rudder was retractable to prevent damage during the beach launch and recovery procedure. Only three other lifeboats were built to this design, which was similar in some respects to the Greathead-built lifeboats of the early 1800s. The second *Benjamin Bond Cabbell* lifeboat was launched on service thirteen times and saved twenty-six lives during her time at Cromer.

Benjamin Bond Cabbell near the pier forecourt as she is pulled along the promenade to try and launch to the west of the pier to help the Norwegian sailing ship *Esras* in March 1901. The ship was stranded at East Runton and her crew was eventually rescued by breeches buoy from the cliff (as pictured below), and the lifeboat was not needed. (Poppyland)

1902-31 • Louisa Heartwell

In April 1901, the RNLI's Committee of Management agreed that a new lifeboat should be sent to Cromer as the old one was deemed unfit for further service. The legacy of £700 bequeathed to the Institution by the late Miss Emily Heartwell, of Upper Holloway, London, was appropriated to the new lifeboat. The committee, coxswain and crew requested a 38ft Liverpool type, fourteen-oared, with a dipping lug, and an order for the new lifeboat was placed with the Thames Iron Works, at Blackwall, London. The Liverpool design was a non-self-righting type intended for sailing, rather than pulling. The new boat was fitted with two water ballast tanks, and two drop keels to give good stability and sailing qualities.

The new lifeboat successfully underwent her harbour trial on 19 July 1902 and, just over a month later, was sent to Cromer. She left Gravesend on 3 September and was towed from the Thames by a tug, with Coxswain James Harrison and a navigating party on board. Taking her to her new station by sea was an unusual occurrence in the era of pulling and sailing lifeboats as they were usually taken to the coast by rail. As *Louisa Heartwell* was a sailing lifeboat, and the journey from London to Cromer relatively short, taking her round by sea was a viable option. During the passage, she gave 'every satisfaction,' according to the District Inspector, and arrived at 7am on 4 September.

The new lifeboat was formally christened five days after she had arrived, but she had to wait more than a year before being called out. Her first service took place in December 1903 when she stood by the steamship *Enriquetta*, of Grangemouth, for three days. Her first life-saving service took place on 10 October 1904 when she was launched to the steamer *Rosalind*, of Newcastle, which had its steering apparatus broken during a gale.

Louisa Heartwell served at Cromer until May 1931, during which time she launched 115 times on service and is credited with saving almost 200 lives. She was sold out of service on 20 May 1931 to Nathaniel Green, of Stiffkey, and converted into a motor cruiser. Renamed *Waiora*, she was kept in Norfolk for a number of years and was later fitted with a 125bhp Chrysler engine. During the 1990s, she became a houseboat on the Chichester Canal.

Louisa Heartwell, pictured on her launching carriage with the crew in their cork life-jackets, was sent to Cromer in September 1902. She was a Liverpool non-self-righting type, 38ft in length, pulling fourteen oars and equipped with a dipping lug. Built by Thames Iron Works at Blackwall, she was generally intended for sailing, rather than rowing.

Louisa Heartwell pictured during her naming and dedication ceremony on the East Beach, 9 September 1902. During the ceremony, Commander Thomas Holmes, RN, the District Inspector, accepted the new boat on behalf of the Institution, and then paid tribute to the role of the crew, saying: 'The steps recently taken to improve the efficiency of the Cromer Lifeboat Station . . . would be of no use unless they had an efficient Lifeboat crew to take care of the boat.' After praising the Coxswain and crew, he then handed over the new boat to Henry Broadhurst, MP, who accepted her on behalf of the local committee. After a short service of dedication, Lady Suffield stepped forward and said, 'I have pleasure in naming this lifeboat *Louisa Heartwell*, and I hope it will save many lives', while breaking the bottle suspended over the bow of the boat. Amid cheers from the crowd, the lifeboat was launched for a short demonstration of her capabilities off the beach. The new lifeboat was funded from a legacy bequeathed to the RNLI by the late Miss Emily Heartwell, of London, who stipulated that she wanted to provide a lifeboat for service on the east coast named *Louisa Heartwell*. (Top photo supplied by Paul Russell; lower photo from Poppyland)

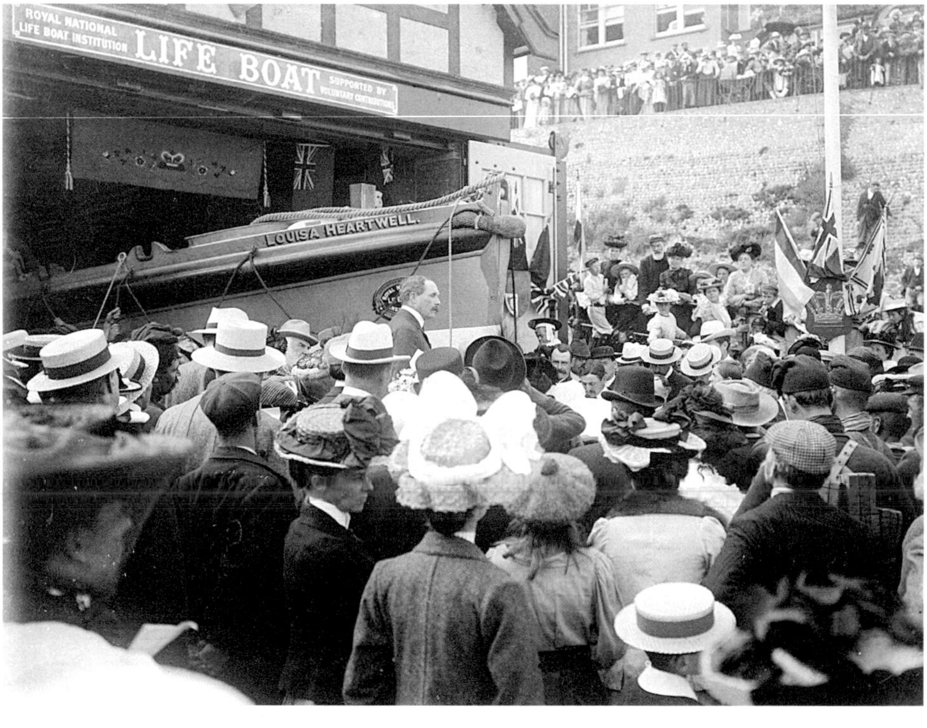

Louisa Heartwell and her crew during the naming and dedication ceremony on 9 September 1902. After the formal speeches, she was launched in front of a large crowd of well-wishers. After the ceremony, the lifeboat crew were guests of honour at the Bath Hotel, Cromer, and were given 'a capital repast'. (Poppyland)

Louisa Heartwell launching from the East Beach off her carriage. (From an old postcard supplied by Paul Russell)

Two pictures of the lifeboat house built in 1868 by the RNLI at the East Gangway. The first lifeboat house at Cromer, in which the lifeboat was kept on 'a four double wheel sliding cradle', had been built by the Norfolk Association about 100 yards from the high water mark and ten yards from the Coastguard cottages. On taking over the station in 1858, the RNLI altered and renovated it, but by the mid-1860s it had become unsuitable and so was replaced. A new site was obtained at the East Gangway in 1864, but it took almost four years for the new house to be completed, with part of its construction involving building an extension to the sea wall and a slipway across the beach. Built by local builder E. Simmons, the new house cost £476.4s.0d, which was defrayed by Benjamin Bond Cabbell who had also bought the new lifeboat for the station, as well as its launching carriage. The house of 1868 served the station until 1902, when a larger lifeboat was sent and a larger house built on the same site. The original lifeboat house was demolished in 1884, having been used as a fishermen's lookout room and library during its final years. (Above: Poppyland photo, left: A. Rogers)

When *Louisa Heartwell* came to Cromer, a new lifeboat house was needed and so this building was completed in 1902 to house the Liverpool type lifeboat and her carriage. The house was used operationally until the 1960s and later became the lifeboat museum. (Courtesy of Tony Rogers)

The lifeboat house of 1902 housed the No.2 lifeboats from 1923 until 1967 and was then used for the inshore lifeboat, subsequently becoming the Henry Blogg Lifeboat Museum, as pictured here. (Nicholas Leach)

Louisa Heartwell being launched in a calm sea, possibly at the end of her naming ceremony as many of those in attendance have early cameras ready to catch the spectacle. Launching from the beach was an operation fraught with difficulties, particularly in severe weather. (Poppyland)

Louisa Heartwell at the foot of the gangway preparing to launch on lifeboat day, 16 August 1923. Although the new motor lifeboat *H. F. Bailey* had recently arrived at Cromer, only *Louisa Heartwell* was launched for the day's public demonstration.

Louisa Heartwell being brought from the East Gangway boathouse for launching in the early 1920s with people gathering to watch and the lifeboat men busy clearing a path for their boat. The breadth of the Liverpool class lifeboat can be appreciated from this photograph, a characteristic that made it a fine seaworthy craft, although it was not self-righting.

Louisa Heartwell under sail. Her sailing abilities meant she could cover a much greater range than if she relied solely on oars and this was an important factor in enabling the lifeboat men to reach casualties on the outlying sandbanks, such as the Haisborough Sands. (From a postcard supplied by Paul Russell)

Pulling away from the beach, *Louisa Heartwell* pictured in July 1924, by which time she had been designated the No.2 lifeboat with the slipway-launched motor lifeboat as the No.1 boat. (By courtesy of P. A. Vicary)

A posed photograph of *Louisa Heartwell* being launched off the beach. While the carriage made getting the boat afloat easier, in heavy surf launching from the beach was often a difficult and dangerous undertaking. (From a postcard supplied by Paul Russell)

A dramatic shot of *Louisa Heartwell* launching from the beach into a rough sea. (From an old postcard supplied by Ros Davies)

Swedish steamship Fernebo

The most famous rescue in which *Louisa Heartwell* was involved took place on 9 January 1917 and resulted in the award of the first of three Gold medals to Coxswain Henry Blogg. Events began after the lfieboat was returning from assisting the Greek steamer *Pyrin*, which got into difficulty riding out the heavy north-easterly gale. Just as the lifeboat was beaching on her return from *Pyrin*, an explosion occurred on board the Swedish steamship *Fernebo*. The explosion in the steamer's boilers broke the vessel in half and the two halves soon separated.

Despite having already been at sea for several hours in difficult conditions, the by now exhausted Cromer crew set out again. Getting the lifeboat clear of the breakers proved to be a considerable struggle and the lifeboatmen were eventually beaten back. Meanwhile, a small boat had left *Fernebo* with six of the steamer's crew. Although this boat was capsized in the surf, somehow all of its six occupants were brought to safety, mainly through the efforts of those on the beach.

By the late afternoon of 9 January, the two halves of the steamer had grounded, one alongside a wooden groyne, and the other a mile further to the east. The rocket apparatus tried to get a line to the stranded parts of the steamer, but the force of the wind made it impossible to get a line across. At 9pm, Coxswain Blogg consulted with Commander Basil Hall, RN, the RNLI's District Inspector, about making another attempt with the lifeboat. Hall consented to a launch, and at 9.30pm the lifeboat put off again.

During the first attempt, five oars were smashed, three more were washed away and Blogg was forced to return to the shore. But Blogg was not to be beaten and, with his brave crew, decided to make another attempt. After a short rest, spare oars were found and for the fourth time that day the lifeboat was launched at a point where the tide had begun to create a current which swept almost out to the wreck. This time they were successful, and *Louisa Heartwell* was brought alongside the wreck long enough for the crew of eleven men, the steamer's entire complement, to be pulled to safety. The lifeboat then returned to shore accompanied by cheering from the crowd. It was just before 1am and Henry Blogg and his crew had been battling the North Sea on and off for fourteen hours.

The dramatic rescue of the *Fernebo's* crew had been an outstanding act of courage and daring and for this extraordinary feat Blogg received the RNLI's Gold medal. The other Cromer lifeboatmen were also formally recognised, some with a new award, the Bronze medal. Acting Second Coxswain William Davies was awarded the Silver medal, twelve of the crew who went out three times the Bronze medal, and six who went out twice were accorded the Thanks on Vellum. The Bronze medal was a new award instituted by the RNLI's committee specifically because of the notable contributions of the Cromer crew during this service and this was the first time it had been presented.

An old postcard depicting *Louisa Heartwell* launching with the wreck of the steamship *Fernebo* in the background. The wreck was not finally removed from the beach until 1922.

Louisa Heartwell on her carriage ready to be launched with a large crowd watching. Note the Tipping's Plates fitted to the wheels of the carriage. These were specially developed for stations where carriage launching was employed and were intended to prevent the wheels from sinking into soft sand. (Poppyland)

Louisa Heartwell returning to the beach ready for recovery.

Louisa Heartwell at Great Yarmouth on 11 February 1910. She was taken to the port several times after services before being sailed back to her station.

Louisa Heartwell preparing to launch on lifeboat day in her later days at Cromer, with the No.1 boathouse and slipway at the end of the pier, background right. (Supplied by Ros Davies)

An excellent photograph of *Louisa Heartwell* on the beach before the new lifeboat station was constructed. During the final six years of her career at Cromer, *Louisa Heartwell* was not called upon to perform any effective services and in 1931, after almost three decades on station, she left Cromer for the last time. The *Eastern Daily Press* on 16 May 1931 reported the event in somewhat dramatic fashion: 'The Louisa Heartwell has gone! Cromer's No.2 lifeboat has been towed to Lowestoft to be sold by public auction – an inglorious end to a glorious career.' The newspaper went on to report that she 'has been the means of saving 206 lives and assisted in helping fifty-two vessels.' A few people watched from the cliffs as the lifeboat departed, being drawn out of the boathouse and across the beach, dragged to the water's edge and launched. The motor lifeboat *H. F. Bailey* then towed *Louisa Heartwell* to Lowestoft where Messrs Hobson & Co sold her on 20 May 1931 by auction. (From an old postcard courtesy of Tony Rogers)

Sold out of service to Nathaniel Green, of Stiffkey, *Louisa Heartwell* was converted by Warfolk Bros at King's Lynn into the motor cruiser *Waiora*. She was initially based on the north Norfolk coast and later moved to Wales, being kept at Aberaeron and Barry Dock. By the 1990s, she was at Rickmansworth and later moved to the Chichester Canal, where she is pictured as a houseboat. (Paul Russell)

1923-35 • Motor lifeboats

The RNLI started trialling motor lifeboats in 1904, when a pulling lifeboat was fitted with an engine. Once the technical difficulties of operating a motor in a lifeboat had been solved, powered lifeboats represented the future for the service, and a building programme of motor lifeboats began. The question of placing a motor lifeboat at Cromer was first raised in October 1917, but not until the following year was a decision taken by the RNLI to supply a motor lifeboat to the station and the boat itself did not arrive until the early 1920s.

Cromer's first motor lifeboat, named *H. F. Bailey*, was based on the Norfolk & Suffolk design of pulling lifeboat, a type developed by the East Anglian beachmen and ideally suited for work in shallow waters due to its relatively flat bottom. The new lifeboat, 46ft 6in in length, was the third of the motorised Norfolk & Suffolk class. She was fitted with an 80hp Weyburn DE.6 engine, and auxiliary sails were also carried. The new lifeboat arrived on 26 May 1923 watched by, according to the *Eastern Daily Press*, 'the greater part of Cromer's population', after a trip during which the engines had proved totally reliable.

To accommodate the motor lifeboat, a new boathouse and slipway were built on the pier. Building work took about three years, and the new lifeboat was hauled up the slipway and into the boathouse for the first time on the day she arrived. She was then launched for the first time, a significant event which involved, according to the local newspaper, 'the boat charging down the slipway and reaching the water with thrilling spectacular effect.'

Between 1923 and 1935, Cromer was served by three motor lifeboats, all named *H. F. Bailey*, having been funded by Henry Francis Bailey, of Brockenhurst, a London merchant born in Norfolk. The first lasted less than a year before being replaced as she was not liked by either the coxswain or crew. The second, a 45ft Watson cabin motor type, arrived in August 1924 and was on station until 1928. Going for refit in 1928, she was replaced by a new 45ft 6in Watson cabin motor type, named *H. F. Bailey II*, which the Cromer crew had the option of keeping. However, after less than six months, they stated that they would prefer their old boat and so the second *H. F. Bailey* returned and remained at the station until December 1935.

Launch of Cromer's first motor lifeboat, the 46ft 6in motorised Norfolk & Suffolk type *H. F. Bailey*, after her naming ceremony on 26 July 1923. During the ceremony, Sir George Shee, Secretary of the RNLI, presented the new lifeboat to the station, and she was dedicated by the Bishop of Norwich. Lady Suffield christened the lifeboat, which was then launched down the new slipway. (From an old postcard supplied by Paul Russell)

Cromer's first motor lifeboat *H. F. Bailey* off the pier on 26 May 1923 with a full complement of Cromer lifeboat men on board. Based on the standard sailing Norfolk & Suffolk type lifeboat, she was essentially an open boat fitted with a single engine which gave her a top speed of more than eight knots. (By courtesy of P. A. Vicary)

A fine photograph of Cromer's first motor lifeboat, *H. F. Bailey*, with sails set, passing the end of the pier. Being single-engined, she also carried a set of sails for use in the event of engine failure. Built at East Cowes at the yard of J. S. White at a cost of almost £11,000, the new lifeboat had a radius of action of forty-five nautical miles at full speed and carried a crew of twelve. (By courtesy of P. A. Vicary)

Line-drawing (below) of the 1923 lifeboat house and slipway built for the station's first motor lifeboat, the outline of which has been included in this architect's drawing. The new house measured 60ft by 21ft internally, with a floor of solid concrete. The advantages of the new house were stated in *The Lifeboat*: 'Now it has a motor lifeboat, Cromer has become one of the most important Stations on the coast, and it was this fact which decided the Institution to make the experiment – for the first time with a Motor Boat – of placing the Boathouse and Slipway at the end of the pier. Here, at all states of the tide, the boat can be launched well clear of all rocks and groynes. The pier itself runs to 500 feet from the shore, and as the boathouse is 60 feet long and the slipway 165 feet, the boat will enter the water nearly 250 yards from the shore.' The problems of launching over the beach, which was obstructed by groynes and occasionally debris from wrecked vessels, were now a thing of the past and the many outstanding rescues performed by the lifeboats operating from this boathouse, described below, vindicated the decision to invest so heavily in the station. The new house, which cost £32,000, meant that a large lifeboat – over 45ft in length – could be operated and one with a far greater range than any pulling lifeboat. (Photo by courtesy of Tony Rogers)

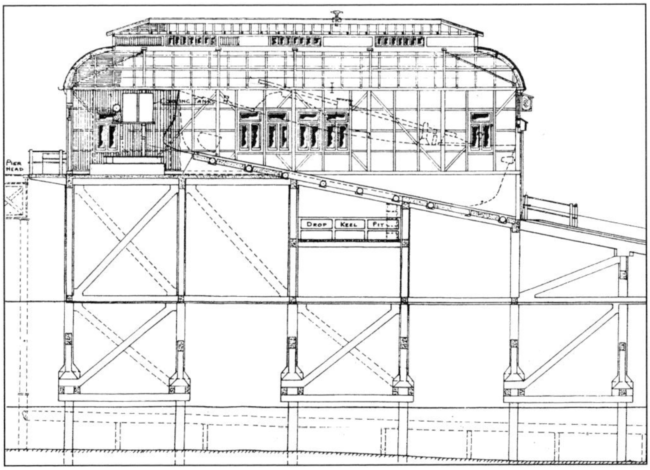

(Right) A rare photo showing the first *H. F. Bailey* on the slipway. During her brief stay at Cromer, she had problems with being both launched and recovered up the slipway and these led to her being transferred to Gorleston in May 1924. (Photo supplied by Ros Davies).

The first motor lifeboat at Cromer, *H. F. Bailey*, alongside the slipway with Coxswain Henry Blogg standing near the stern and looking over the mast. This lifeboat was at Cromer for only a year and was replaced because the friction between her metal keel and the groove in the slipway was so great that she sometimes would not slide down. She is credited with launching three times on service and saving twelve lives during her short career at Cromer. She was sent to the Great Yarmouth & Gorleston station where she served with distinction until 1939, and was then transferred to the Reserve Fleet. She was sold out of service in October 1952. (By courtesy of P. A. Vicary)

H. F. Bailey, the station's second motor lifeboat, on the slipway with the lifeboat crew and helpers. She was a 45ft Watson motor type which the Institution had originally offered to Cromer but which the lifeboatmen had rejected in favour of a Norfolk and Suffolk type. However, problems with the first *H. F. Bailey*, described above, meant she could not be used at Cromer because launching down the slipway was too risky. The new Watson lifeboat arrived on 19 August 1924, having been sailed from Cowes, where she had been built by J. S. White, with Coxswain Blogg accompanied by Captain Carver, District Inspector of Lifeboats, and some of the Cromer lifeboatmen. Built at a cost £7,579 16s 3d, she was fitted with a single 80bhp White DE six-cylinder petrol engine, and during trials had reached a maximum speed of 8.18 knots. (From an old postcard supplied by Paul Russell)

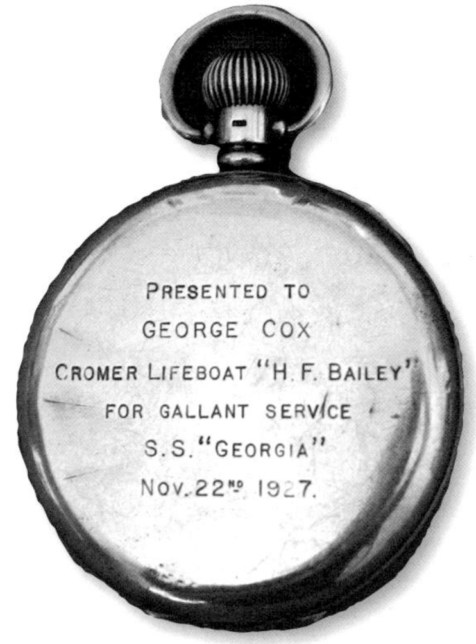

Oil tanker Georgia

The most outstanding rescue in which the second *H. F. Bailey* lifeboat was involved took place in 1927 after the Dutch oil tanker *Georgia*, of Rotterdam, was caught by a vicious gale in the North Sea on 21 November. She struck the Haisborough Sands and was ripped apart amidships by heavy seas. The two halves then drifted away from each other, with fifteen in the fo'c'sle watching sixteen others on the aft part float away.

The next morning, the steamer *Trent* spotted the after part and took off the sixteen men, while news of the stranded vessel reached Great Yarmouth and the Gorleston lifeboat *John and Mary Meiklam of Gladswood* put off. Meanwhile, at about 2pm, *H. F. Bailey* was launched into the easterly gale after the abandoned stern half had been seen off Cromer, but found no sign of life on board. The lifeboat stood by the wreck throughout a bitterly cold night to warn shipping of the danger.

But the Cromer crew did not realise that this was only half the vessel, with the other half in grave danger on the Sands, battered incessantly by the heavy seas, while the Gorleston lifeboat stood by. On 22 November, two tugs, *George Jewson* and *Tactful*, went to help *Georgia*, while the Gorleston lifeboat, under Coxswain Fleming, tried to go alongside, but in the heavy seas all attempts to help failed.

At Cromer, *H. F. Bailey* was being rehoused after standing by the stern section of the tanker when word was received that their services were again required on the Sands. They launched at 1.30pm, taking oil to pour on the sea. At 4.30pm, with daylight fading, *H. F. Bailey* and her crew got sufficiently near the wreck to effect a rescue. As they arrived at the casualty, one of the cargo tanks burst open, spreading oil over the seas and calming them. Coxswain Blogg acted quickly, taking advantage of the relatively smooth seas created by the oil spill, and steered the lifeboat close to the vessel.

As she approached, a heavy sea caught the lifeboat, turned her round and threw her stern against the wreck. She suffered considerable damage, but remained seaworthy enough for the lifeboat crew to throw lines to the stranded men to hold the lifeboat in position. Each time the lifeboat lifted on a swell, one or two of the tanker's crew leapt to safety. Just as all were aboard, the lifeboat was caught by another heavy sea which drove her into the tanker. The engines were slammed into reverse and the lifeboat moved astern, clearing the wreck just in time to avoid serious damage. A course was set for Great Yarmouth.

During this extraordinary rescue, the lifeboat had made no fewer than three trips to the Sands, but perseverence and bravery enabled a dangerous and daring rescue to be completed successfully.

(Above left) The crew of *H. F. Bailey* having just returned from the service to the oil tanker *Georgia*, November 1927. They are, left to right: Jack Davies (snr), George Cox, George Balls, Dick Barker, Jimmy Davies, Jack Davies (jnr), Leslie Harrison, 'Swank' Davies, Coxswain Henry Blogg, Bob Davies, 'Primo' Allen and 'Captain' Davies. Blogg was awarded the Gold medal for this rescue, and the crew each given Bronze medals.

(Above right) Following the *Georgia* service, a public subscription was started and each member of the crew was given an inscribed silver watch, with Blogg receiving a Gold watch. The watches were presented at Cromer Town Hall on 30 January 1928. (Watch supplied by William Cox)

This excellent photo taken of *H. F. Bailey* (second) off the slipway in 1924 clearly shows the layout of the RNLI's early motor lifeboats. The 45ft Watson type was one of the first motor lifeboat classes to have any kind of crew shelter. (By courtesy of P. A. Vicary)

The third lifeboat for the station to be funded from the legacy of Henry Bailey was, somewhat confusingly, named *H. F. Bailey II*. She arrived in December 1928 to replace the second *H. F. Bailey*, which was removed because she had sustained damage during the service to the tanker *Georgia* in November 1927. Built by S. E. Saunders at Cowes, *H. F. Bailey II* served at the station for less than six months, during which time she launched only three times on service and saved five lives. (By courtesy of P. A. Vicary)

The 45ft 6in Watson cabin motor type *H. F. Bailey II* launching down the slipway during her short spell at Cromer. (By courtesy of P. A. Vicary)

H. F. Bailey II passing the slipway with her mast down. The crew had the option of retaining this lifeboat but they preferred their old boat, the second *H. F. Bailey*, which was returned to the station in May 1929 from overhaul. After her brief stint at Cromer, *H. F. Bailey II* was transferred to Selsey where, renamed *Canadian Pacific*, she served as that station's first motor lifeboat. She was destroyed in a fire at Groves & Guttridge boatyard in Cowes on 8 June 1937 during a refit. (By courtesy of P. A. Vicary)

Sir Godfrey Baring presenting Henry Blogg with the RNLI's Silver medal following the service to the cargo ship *Monte Nevoso*. The ceremony, which took place in the Parish Hall on Friday 27 January 1933, also included the presentation of Vellum Certificates to the other twelve members of the crew of the *H. F. Bailey*.

Cargo ship Monte Nevoso

On 14 October 1932, the 5,000-ton cargo ship *Monte Nevoso*, of Genoa, became stranded in fine weather on the Haisborough Sands, fourteen miles from Cromer. Captain Angelino Salvatore and his crew attempted to free her using the steamer's engines, but when this failed he requested the help of tugs. At 9.30am *H. F. Bailey* launched and found the tug *Noordzee* standing by. Five more tugs arrived and attempted to tow the steamer off the sands. But the wind increased and, by the early hours of 15 October, a gale was blowing with heavy seas hampering the rescue attempts. None of the tugs could help and left the steamer as she was about to break up, being banged on the Sands.

Coxswain Blogg then took the lifeboat, which had been standing by for eighteen hours, towards the casualty. *H. F. Bailey* was anchored and veered alongside to take off the steamer's crew. The seamen jumped just as the lifeboat reached the peak of its rise. Several times the lifeboat hit the side of the steamer and, although fenders were used, the boat suffered much damage.

After an hour, twenty-nine of the steamer's crew had been rescued, clambering onto the lifeboat one by one. The Captain and three others, however, refused to leave and so the lifeboat headed for Gorleston to land the survivors. After being refuelled, and the crew changing into dry clothes, the lifeboat put out again at 2pm, but found the Captain still refusing to abandon his vessel, so the lifeboat was forced to return to Gorleston.

At 5am on 16 October Coxswain Blogg took the lifeboat out again. The vessel had by this time broken her back and the four men had abandoned her in the steamer's motor boat. They had left two dogs. One, a large St Bernard, was rescued by the lifeboatmen but the other, a small dog, would not allow itself to be caught and was left behind. The four men who had abandoned the vessel were picked up by a trawler, while Coxswain Blogg took the lifeboat back to Cromer, having been away for nearly fifty-two hours. For this arduous and difficult rescue, Blogg was awarded the Silver medal, and each of the twelve lifeboat crew was accorded the Thanks of the Institution on Vellum.

The motor barge *Goldcrown* ashore at East Runton on the evening of 20 November 1933 with *H. F. Bailey* standing by. The lifeboat, which launched to stand by as the master did not want to abandon ship, passed a hawser between the motor barge and a tug which attempted to tow the barge clear. When this failed and as the barge was in no danger, the lifeboat returned to station after fourteen hours on scene. The barge later refloated and resumed her course. (From a postcard supplied by Paul Russell)

On 13 December 1933, the Dover barge *Sepoy* went aground on Cromer beach and the subsequent rescue turned out to be one of the most famous in the history of Cromer lifeboat station. A series of photographs, taken by local photographers P. A. Vicary and H. H. Tansley, dramatically depict the bravery of the Cromer lifeboat men and undoubtedly helped to bring national recognition to both the town and the station. This photograph shows a rocket carrying a line flying through the air towards the wreck.

Barge Sepoy

In December 1933, when heavy snowstorms swept England and the country was lashed by gale force winds, the Dover barge *Sepoy*, of sixty-five tons, was driven ashore at Cromer. When *Sepoy* hoisted distress signals at dawn, the lifeboat *H. F. Bailey* was on service further down the coast, under Coxswain Heny Blogg, and was on her way to Gorleston as rehousing up the slipway was too dangerous in the conditions.

By 11am, *Sepoy* was dragging her anchors and had started drifting towards the shore. Attempts were made to get the No.2 pulling lifeboat *Alexandra* afloat, with more than 100 people assisting as a cold, biting east-south-east gale blew along the beach. She did get away three times, but each time, despite the best efforts of the crew at their oars, the wind proved too strong and the lifeboat was forced to return to the beach. The Cromer Life Saving Company attempted to save them by firing a rope to the stranded barge. Unfortunately, when a rope was secured to the mast, *Alexandra* drifted over it and cut it in two. The lifeboat was carried past the wreck, over the breakwater and for the third and final time she was flung onto the beach near the boathouse.

Meanwhile, the position of the two men in the *Sepoy's* rigging was getting ever more precarious as all efforts to save them had failed, leaving the only hope of rescue with the No.1 lifeboat. The Coastguard had tried in vain to contact her and only when she was eight miles from Great Yarmouth harbour, at 11.30am, was the Gorleston lifeboat able to relate the plight of *Sepoy* to Blogg. *H. F. Bailey* was nearly twenty miles from Cromer at this point, and had to battle through terrible seas for just over three hours to reach the scene.

At 2.45pm, with the barge 200 yards from Cromer beach and the two men on board having to climb ever higher up the rigging, the motor lifeboat was seen approaching. Fifteen minutes after arriving at Cromer, to the accompaniment of loud cheers from hundreds of onlookers, Coxswain Blogg and his crew succeeded where the pulling boat had failed. Unable to anchor to windward and drop down to the barge, Blogg manoeuvred the lifeboat alongside *Sepoy* with big seas sweeping over her. On the two approaches, the force of water was more powerful than the engines and the lifeboat was swept past the wreck.

When his third approach also failed, Blogg realised drastic action was needed. So, after shouting orders to the crew and the mechanics to be ready for action, he circled the barge and, from the lee side, pointed the lifeboat's bow at the barge and drove straight at the wreck. He took the boat right on top of the barge, close to the rigging where the men were hanging and, with the lifeboat in an extremely hazardous position, the first man was dragged to safety. Before the second man, Captain Hemstead, could be saved, a sea lifted the lifeboat and swept her off the wreck. Blogg was therefore forced to drive the boat over the barge for a second time to complete the rescue.

Despite being damaged during this operation, *H. F. Bailey* was driven onto the beach where the two men were landed. Blogg had decided that a long passage to Gorleston was too risky for the survivors and, with the lifeboat short of fuel, beaching was a better option. As soon as the lifeboat grounded, a dozen men ran into the sea to steady her while others helped the survivors. One was taken ashore on a stretcher while the Captain went to the Red Lion Hotel. The crowd cheered the lifeboatmen and acclaimed Coxswain Blogg, who praised his own 'magnificent' crew. The official account concluded: 'It was a dangerous service, carried out in the worst weather, on a lee shore in very heavy surf, where there was continual risk that the lifeboat herself would be washed up on the beach. That the two men were rescued and the lifeboat was not wrecked was due to the seamanship of the coxswain.'

The remains of the wrecked barge *Sepoy* on Cromer beach at low tide on 14 December 1933, the day after the dramatic rescue. (By courtesy of P. A. Vicary)

During the rescue efforts, the No.2 lifeboat *Alexandra* was dragged along the beach to go to the aid of the grounded *Sepoy* as, with the No.1 lifeboat elsewhere, she was the only hope for the barge's stranded crew. With the barge in serious difficulties, further rockets were fired but without success. This photograph shows *Alexandra* on her carriage being made ready for launching through the surf, but she was unable to get close to the wreck in the heavy seas.

The No.1 lifeboat *H. F. Bailey* succeeded where the pulling boat failed and rescued the two men from the barge's rigging after being driven over the wreck by Coxswain Blogg in one of the most daring pieces of seamanship ever witnessed. The lifeboat left the wreck five minutes later and was beached in front of crowds of onlookers as the barge was overwhelmed by the seas and sunk. This very rare postcard has been signed by the skipper of *Sepoy*, Joseph Hempstead, as well as Coxswain Blogg. (From an old postcard supplied by David Gooch)

The service to the barge *Sepoy* by the Cromer motor lifeboat was one of the finest services in the history of the Cromer station. The *Eastern Daily Press* of 14 December 1933, in recounting the 'thrilling rescue', stated that 'so fine was the seamanship shown by Coxswain Blogg and his crew that by way of celebration a peal was rung on the Cromer Church bells.' The crew of the No.1 lifeboat *H. F. Bailey* who took part in the rescue, pictured on the beach with the lifeboat, 13 December 1933, were, left to right: Coxswain Henry Blogg and his dog Monte, Walter Allen, H. W. 'Swank' Davies, Jimmy Davies, George Balls, W. H. 'Pimpo' Davies, Lewis 'Tuna' Harrison, Bowman Jack Davies, William 'Captain' Davies, Bob 'Skinback' Cox and Charlie Cox. For his extraordinary courage and outstanding seamanship, Coxswain Blogg was awarded a second-service clasp to his Silver medal, and each of the crew was accorded the Thanks of the Institution inscribed on Vellum. Robert Davies, acting coxswain of the No.2 lifeboat, was also accorded the Thanks of the Institution on Vellum. (From an old postcard supplied by Paul Russell)

(Right) Bob 'Ridley' Davies standing next to the beached *H. F. Bailey* following the *Sepoy* service. Bob Davies had taken charge of the No.2 lifeboat, *Alexandra*, during her three launches to the stricken barge, and he was awarded the Institution's Thanks on Vellum for his efforts. He had been the mechanic of the *H. F. Bailey* until October 1933, when he was forced to retire due to eyesight problems. (Photo supplied by Ros Davies)

H. F. Bailey launching in rough weather on 16 May 1935, towards the end of her service at Cromer. After leaving the station in December 1935, she served as a reserve lifeboat for more than two decades, including twice returning to Cromer during the war and launching a further seven times, until being sold out of service in September 1953. (By courtesy of P. A. Vicary)

H. F. Bailey off the slipway in June 1935 after picking up the body of Charlie Cox, whose crab boat *White Heather* had overturned. (By courtesy of P. A. Vicary)

H. F. Bailey launching down the slipway. In this photo, the single tunnel in which the propeller was housed can clearly be seen. (By courtesy of P. A. Vicary)

Reserve 45ft Watson motor lifeboat *City of Bradford I* launching on exercise during one of her periods on duty at Cromer, either June 1931 or June 1932. (By courtesy of P. A. Vicary)

1935-45 • The last H. F. Bailey

In the mid-1930s, Cromer was sent two new motor lifeboats. In 1934, a new No.2 lifeboat was supplied, and the following year a new No.1 lifeboat was placed on station. The new No.1 lifeboat, the fourth to carry the name *H. F. Bailey*, arrived on 15 December 1935 and was watched by a large crowd as she was hauled up the slipway. As she reached the boathouse for the first time, the exhaust funnel was found to be an inch or so too tall to get under the top of the door, so part of it had to be removed to give more clearance; a new, smaller funnel was supplied later.

Built at a cost of £7,307, the new lifeboat was a Watson cabin motor type, similar to her predecessor but slightly larger at 46ft in length. Her hull was divided into seven watertight compartments, of which the engine room was one, and fitted with 142 air cases. Manned by a crew of twelve, she carried the latest equipment, which included a line-throwing gun and an electric searchlight. Most significant of all, however, were her engines: twin 40hp Weyburn CE.4 four-cylinder diesel engines gave her a maximum speed of just over eight knots and, at a cruising speed of 7.5 knots, she had a range of almost 100 nautical miles. Twin engines meant that the need to carry sails was obviated, while the diesel engine was more economical to operate than its petrol counterpart and thus increased the range of the lifeboat.

Having been operational at Cromer for some time, the new lifeboat was formally christened at the pier boathouse on 27 August 1937 at an unusual double ceremony which also saw the new No.2 lifeboat *Harriot Dixon* named. With Lord Suffield, president of the Branch, in the chair, Sir Geoffrey Baring, chairman of the RNLI, presented the lifeboats to the station on behalf of the donors and the Institution. The Bishop of Norwich, the Right Reverend Bertram Pollock, conducted the service of dedication, after which the lifeboats were christened by the Rt Hon Sir Samuel Hoare, MP, and *H. F. Bailey* was launched down the slipway for a demonstration with the No.2 lifeboat.

During ten years of service at Cromer, *H. F. Bailey* completed more than 150 service launches and saved an impressive 518 lives, being involved in some of the station's most outstanding rescues. After Cromer, she served at Helvick Head for fourteen years and was sold in June 1973 for display at Thorpe Water Park in Middlesex. As one of the most famous lifeboats ever to serve the RNLI, she was returned to Cromer in the 1990s, and is now on display as the centrepiece of the Henry Blogg Lifeboat Museum.

46ft Watson *H. F. Bailey* at the foot of the slipway as she arrives on station, 15 December 1935. She reached Cromer shortly after 11am and a large crowd watched her being rehoused for the first time. She had left Cowes on 12 December and came to Cromer via Newhaven, Ramsgate and Gorleston. (From a postcard supplied by Roger Wiltshire)

The fourth *H. F. Bailey* (ON.777) arrives at Cromer, 15 December 1935. Coxswain Blogg was in command during the voyage from Cowes, accompanied by Lifeboat Inspector Commander P. E. Vaux, Honorary Secretary E. Peter Hansell and Colonel F. Noel, a member of the Cromer Committee. (By courtesy of P. A. Vicary)

The 46ft Watson cabin motor *H. F. Bailey* arrives at Cromer, 15 December 1935, having set off from her builder's yard at Cowes three days earlier. (By courtesy of P. A. Vicary)

H. F. Bailey is recovered up the slipway for the first time following her arrival on station in December 1935. During this first recovery, the exhaust funnel was found to be an inch or so too high to get under the top of the door, so part of the funnel had to be removed to give the necessary clearance with a new, slightly smaller funnel supplied later. (By courtesy of P. A. Vicary)

Although *H. F. Bailey* had an unequalled war record while at Cromer, controversy also played a part during those years. In April 1942 Coxswain Henry Blogg, along with other members of the crew, threatened to resign from the lifeboat service after two of his nephews, twenty-year-old cousins Robert Charles 'Bob' Davies and James Richard 'Dick' Davies, were called up for war service and it was suggested that men from the Labour Exchange should be trained as crew. Blogg was opposed to the idea of non-seafaring crew, and several lifeboatmen had already been enlisted in the armed forces. To resolve the situation, meetings were held between the local MP Sir Thomas Cook, representatives from the Ministry of Labour and the RNLI, and although the two men were enlisted in the Navy, from then on crew members over twenty-one had their call-ups deferred and stayed in Cromer. (By courtesy of P. A. Vicary)

H. F. Bailey being launched down the slipway, August 1937. (By courtesy of P. A. Vicary)

The

Royal National Life-boat Institution

(Supported solely by Voluntary Contributions)

INAUGURAL CEREMONY

OF THE

MOTOR LIFE-BOATS

"H. F. BAILEY"

AND

"HARRIOT DIXON"

Cromer Motor Life-boat rescues the crew of the barge *Sepoy*, 13th December, 1933.

at

THE PIER PAVILION, CROMER.

on

FRIDAY, AUGUST 27th, 1937, at 3 p.m.

The Naming Ceremony to be performed by

The Right Hon. SIR SAMUEL HOARE, Bt.,

P.C., G.C.S.I., G.B.E., C.M.G., M.P., Secretary of State for Home Affairs.

The *H. F. Bailey* has been built out of a legacy from the late Mr. H. F. Bailey, of Brockenhurst, Hants., and the *Harriot Dixon* out of a legacy from the late Mr. W. E. Dixon, of West Worthing, Sussex. The searchlight of the *H. F. Bailey* is a gift from the Mitcham Schools, Surrey, and the compass from supporters of the Institution in Warsaw.

(Above left) *H. F. Bailey* launches at the end of her naming ceremony on 27 August 1937.

(Above right) *H. F. Bailey* at sea with *Harriot Dixon* following the double naming ceremony for both boats. The unusual ceremony was held at the pier boathouse with Lord Suffield, president of the Branch, in the chair. Sir Geoffrey Baring, chairman of the RNLI, presented the lifeboats to the station and they were received by Lt Col F. A. G. Noel, chairman of the Branch. The Bishop of Norwich, the Rt Rev Bertram Pollock, conducted a service of dedication, after which the lifeboats were named by the Rt Hon Sir Samuel Hoare, Bt, MP, Secretary of State for Home Affairs. *H. F. Bailey*, built at a cost of £7,307, was the fourth and final lifeboat to be provided through the estate of the late Henry Francis Bailey, of Brockenhurst. The boat's searchlight was funded by a gift from the Mitcham Schools, Surrey, and her compass was provided out of gifts from RNLI supporters in Warsaw and received through the British Embassy there.

(Left) The ceremony programme included the names of both lifeboats for what was an unusual event. The picture shows a painting of the second *H. F. Bailey* rescuing the crew of the barge *Sepoy* by R. A. Dixon.

A fine photograph of *H. F. Bailey*, showing the layout of the 46ft Watson cabin motor with its aft cockpit, but with the funnel shortened to fit in the boathouse at Cromer. (By courtesy of P. A. Vicary)

A dramatic launch for *H. F. Bailey* into a north-easterly gale on 10 February 1938. She put out to two fishing boats caught out in a gale force wind, and stood by one, *Urgent*, of Cowes, until it was safely beached at Overstrand. (By courtesy of P. A. Vicary)

H. F. Bailey at Robinson's Yard, Oulton Broad, for repairs following the service to Convoy 559 in August 1941. During the service, she was severely damaged having twice been driven over sunken decks, been bumped severely on the sands, and at one point been run aground. About 20ft of her port fender had been torn off, her stem had been damaged, and the bolts had been forced right through six or eight inches of the deadwood and punctured some of the air cases inside the hull. A plaque (below) commemorating the rescue is on display in the boathouse at the end of the pier.

Convoy 559

On 5 August 1941, a convoy of merchant ships, escorted by naval vessels, was making its way down the east coast through a north-north-westerly gale. During the early hours of 6 August, the convoy was off the Norfolk coast when six of the steamers, *Oxshott* of London, *Deerwood* of London, *Gallois* of Rouen, *Taara* of Parmu, *Aberhill* of Methil, and *Betty Hendly* were driven onto the Haisborough Sands. When news of the stranding reached Cromer, *H. F. Bailey* put out under the command of Coxswain Henry Blogg and an hour and forty minutes later reached the Sands to find the seas breaking over the stranded steamers.

H. F. Bailey made first for *Oxshott*, which had only her masts, funnel and upper works above the water. Sixteen men, roped together, were hanging behind the vessel's funnel and so Coxswain Blogg immediately made for a wedge-shaped opening, taking the lifeboat over the submerged deck and onto the vessel. The sea kept washing the lifeboat away, but again and again the boat's bow was forced into the opening and held there until all sixteen men had been hauled to safety.

Blogg then took the lifeboat alongside the second steamer, *Gallois*, and using the lifeboat's engines held her alongside while some of the steamer's crew jumped aboard and others slid down ropes. *H. F. Bailey* rescued thirty-one men from *Gallois* and then left the sands to transfer the forty-seven rescued men to a destroyer.

H. F. Bailey then approached the third steamer, *Deerwood*, which had only her bridge above water. Blogg drove the lifeboat over the steamer's bulwarks and the submerged deck and held the lifeboat against the bridge while the nineteen crew jumped aboard. With three crews now rescued, Blogg and his crew made for a fourth ship, *Aberhill*, but found the Great Yarmouth and Gorleston lifeboat *Louise Stephens* had arrived and was already engaged in a rescue. So *H. F. Bailey* went on to *Taara*, but the No.2 lifeboat *Harriot Dixon* was already alongside her. *H. F. Bailey* went to the sixth of the steamers, *Betty Hendly*, which had also had her back broken. Blogg took the lifeboat alongside and the twenty-two men of the crew jumped aboard.

As a result of this series of outstanding rescues, the RNLI awarded Coxswain Blogg a second service clasp to his Gold medal. Silver medals went to Second Coxswain John J. Davies, who took command of *Harriot Dixon*, and to Coxswain Charles Johnson of Great Yarmouth and Gorleston. The Bronze medal was awarded to three other Cromer lifeboatmen: Second Coxswain Leslie Harrison, in *Harriot Dixon*, and the two mechanics, Henry Davies and H. V. Linder.

English Trader

In October 1941, Coxswain Blogg and the crew of the Cromer lifeboat were involved in one of the most outstanding rescues of the Second World War. This service, to the steamer *English Trader*, has become one of the most famous of all the rescues performed by Blogg despite the fact that he was not awarded the Gold medal for his efforts. During this service, the lifeboatmen were pushed to the limit and tragically one of their own did lose his life.

The 1934-built steamship *English Trader* was part of Convoy EC90 sailing from the Thames to the Firth of Forth. On 25 October the convoy formed and began its journey up the east coast. As she was steaming slowly through the channel between Hammond Knoll and the Haisborough Sands, between 1am and 1.30am on 26 October, *English Trader* found herself in the grip of a strong ebbtide and, unknown to her crew, the strength of the tide had in fact pushed the ship aground.

By daybreak, the weather was rapidly worsening and the wind had reached gale force. The ship's boats could not be got away in the turbulent seas running on the sandbank, and the crew were stranded. Reports of the vessel's plight were recieved at Cromer and, at 8.15am on 26 October, *H. F. Bailey* was launched into the gale, with heavy squalls of rain, hail and sleet making conditions extremely cold. When the lifeboat reached Hammond Knoll at 11.35am, *English Trader* was found with little more than her masts, funnel and chart-room above water and forty-four men stranded on board. Five others had been swept overboard and drowned before the lifeboat arrived.

In the terrible conditions, with the seas not running true and the steamer's derricks swinging about, getting the lifeboat alongside was impossible. As Blogg attempted to get to the lee side of the steamer despite very heavy seas coming round both bow and stern, a huge wall of water suddenly rose up and overwhelmed his boat. She was tossed over, almost capsized, and Blogg, Second Coxswain Jack Davies and three other crew members were thrown overboard. As the boat came upright, the Second Coxswain's son brought the boat under control, and went to pick up the other men in the water. It proved very difficult actually getting them on board as they were so waterlogged, and signalman Edward Allen, the last to be rescued, was unconscious by the time the lifeboat reached him. Once aboard the lifeboat, he was revived and sat up, spoke a few words, but then suddenly collapsed and died.

After this, Blogg decided to make at once for Great Yarmouth, while the Gorleston lifeboat *Louise Stephens* went to the steamer. She made five separate attempts to go alongside but, being heavily buffeted, failed to get alongside as the Cromer boat had done. With the seas increasing and darkness setting in, the captain of *English Trader* waved the lifeboat to go away.

The Cromer lifeboat reached Yarmouth, where a doctor and an ambulance were waiting, and the body of the signalman was landed. The boat was refuelled, the crew given hot food and new clothes and, just after 4am on 27 October, *H. F. Bailey* put to sea again. It took three hours and twenty minutes to reach the sands, but by then both wind and sea were much lighter.

The fore part of *English Trader* was now under water, but the lifeboat was able to go alongside the steamer's lee rail, which was only about two feet above her. Within half an hour the forty-four survivors of the crew had been taken on board and the lifeboat was making again for Great Yarmouth.

For this truly remarkable rescue, Coxswain Blogg was awarded a third clasp to the Silver medal and each of the crew was awarded the Bronze medal. They also received a copy of the vote inscribed on vellum and a pension was granted to Edward Allen's widow on the same scale as if he had been a sailor killed in action.

The five lifeboatmen washed overboard during the *English Trader* rescue were, from left to right, Coxswain Henry Blogg, Henry 'Shrimp' Davies, Sidney Charles 'Kelly' Harrison, Edward Walter 'Primo' Allen and John James 'Jack' Davies.

H. F. Bailey, official number 777, was well liked by Blogg and his crew in her relatively short time at Cromer. Her number was thought to be particularly lucky to the superstitious fishermen who manned her, and she certainly rode her luck during the *English Trader* service. An impressive record of 154 launches and 448 lives saved is unlikely to be bettered at Cromer.

H. F. Bailey during a publicity trip to Bristol in the early 1970s. (By courtesy of the RNLI)

H. F. Bailey's 'final' trip took place on 9 November 1973 when she was taken along the Thames from Greenwich to Tower Pier to HMS *Belfast*. She was commanded by Cdr Harold Harvey, the only RNLI Inspector to be awarded the Gold medal, with two former Moelfre lifeboat men, double gold medal winner Coxswain Richard Evans and ex-Mechanic/Second Coxswain Evan Owen, also on board. They were attending a reception on board the former RN cruiser.

1945-67 • Post-war lifeboats

Shortly after the Second World War had ended, a new lifeboat arrived at Cromer. Named *Millie Walton*, she was sent from her builder's via Gorleston on 20 December 1945 and, after a series of trials and practice runs, was hauled up the slipway at Cromer and successfully housed. She was a 46ft 9in twin screw Watson class lifeboat, with a hull shape similar to her predecessor but with a forward steering position. Her machinery installation consisted of twin Ferry VE.4 four-cylinder diesels, each of 40bhp, giving a maximum speed of 8.22 knots. She was built by the Sussex Shipbuilding Co, of Shoreham, and was funded from the legacy of Mrs M. E. Walton, of Derby.

Originally sent to Cromer on a temporary basis, the new design was to be tried out by the Cromer crew, regarded as one of the most experienced in the country, but as Coxswain Blogg and the crew liked her so much they asked for her to be stationed permanently at Cromer. The Institution agreed to this request and allocated its general funds to pay for the boat so that she could be renamed *Henry Blogg* in honour of the town's most famous lifeboat men.

The naming ceremony of the new lifeboat had to be delayed because the pier was not considered safe for a large number of people as it was undergoing renovation, and major repairs to the slipway during summer 1947 put it out of action. On 7 August 1948, the new lifeboat was finally named, being formally christened by Admiral of the Fleet Sir John Cunningham. She was named after Cromer's most famous coxswain, who had retired in September 1947, and had been presented with a portrait of himself by T. C. Dugdale, RA, and a framed certificate of service. *Henry Blogg* gave more than two decades of service at Cromer, during which time she saved almost 150 lives and launched almost 100 times on service.

A fine study of Cromer's first post-war lifeboat, the 46ft Watson cabin motor *Henry Blogg* (ON.840), one of the first lifeboats to be built with a midship steering position. She was one of only five lifeboats to be built at Shoreham by the Sussex Shipbuilding Company.

Millie Walton at the Sussex Shipbuilding Co boatyard where she was built. She was one of only five lifeboats built by this firm and had originally been allocated to Douglas, Isle of Man. (By courtesy of P. Poulter)

Millie Walton left her builder's yard at Shoreham for her new station on 14 December 1945. During the passage, she called at Gorleston on 19 December 1945, having put into Lowestoft earlier in the day to pick up the Gorleston Coxswain and Mechanic and the Lowestoft Coxswain. This picture shows her arriving at Gorleston. She eventually reached Cromer on Thursday 20 December 1945.

The 46ft Watson cabin motor lifeboat *Millie Walton* (ON.840) at Cromer before she was renamed *Henry Blogg*, a name given to her in July 1946. She was built in 1945 and was originally allocated to Douglas, coming to Cromer initially on a temporary basis only. (By courtesy of P. A. Vicary)

Henry Blogg immediately after launching to go to the aid of the steamer *Francois Tixier,* which capsized off Sheringham in July 1948. (By courtesy of P. A. Vicary)

Steamship Francois Tixier

On 8 July 1948 the 650-ton French steamer *Francois Tixier*, bound from Goole to Rouen with a cargo of coal, capsized in heavy seas about four miles off Sheringham. With the Sheringham lifeboat undergoing refit at Oulton Broad, *Henry Blogg* was launched to the steamer's aid and stood by the casualty in a worsening gale. With the steamer heavily listing to port, the lifeboat went alongside but the captain and crew refused to leave. As the cargo shifted further to port, and the ship's crew failed in their attempt to steady their vessel, they agreed to leave. One man jumped into the water and was picked up, while the next reached the lifeboat via a rope passed from the ship.

Then, using the breeches buoy, eight more men were taken off the steamer which, by this time, was rolling on her beam ends. After an eleventh man was taken off using the breeches buoy, five remained on the casualty. At this point, the steamer rolled right over and settled down under the water with the last five men standing on the stern. As they went into the water, a raft came floating away from the ship into which they climbed to be picked up by the lifeboat shortly afterwards. The lifeboat then headed through heavy seas to reach Great Yarmouth, where the sixteen rescued French seamen were landed.

Coxswain Davies commented with a degree of modesty, 'It was a nice job perhaps, but we have done bigger ones. Please don't make too much fuss about it.' In recognition of their efforts and seamanship during this rescue, the crew were presented with awards by the French Government.

Henry Blogg arriving at Great Yarmouth with the survivors from the steamer *Francois Tixier*, 8 July 1948. Once the survivors had been landed, the lifeboat men went to a quayside café at Gorleston for hot drinks and then returned home by motor coach, leaving the lifeboat until the weather was calm enough for rehousing. In recognition of the efforts of the lifeboat men, and their display of good seamanship during this rescue, they were presented with awards by the French Government. On 13 September 1949, Capitaine de Corvette de la Loge d'Ausson, Commanding Officer of the French fishery protection vessel, *Ailette*, made the presentations during a special ceremony held in the town. Coxswain Davies received the French Maritime Cross and Diploma and each of the other eleven members of the crew a French life-saving medal inscribed with the name of the recipient and containing the words 'Courage and Devotion'. The recipients were Second Coxswain Lewis Harrison, Bowman R. C. Davies, Mechanic H. W. Davies, Assistant Mechanic L. J. Harrison, Signaller F. Davies and Messrs. S. C. Harrison, J. J. Davies, J. R. Davies. G. Cox, G. Rook and T. Jonas. (By courtesy of Eastern Counties Newspapers)

(Above) Presentation on 13 September 1949 of French awards for the *Francois Tixier* service. Pictured left to right, front row, 'Bob' Davies, H. W. 'Swank' Davies and Henry Davies; middle row, George Rook, Lewis 'Tuna' Harrison, L. J. Harrison, S. C. Harrison; and back row, J. R. Davies, J. J. Davies, George Cox, Tom Jonas and Frank Davies.

Henry Blogg on the slipway for her naming ceremony in August 1948. The ceremony was a major event in the town and the events of the day were described by the *Eastern Daily Press*: 'With a record of fifty-three years as a lifeboat man, during thirty-eight of which he was coxswain at Cromer, Mr Henry George Blogg was the chief figure in the naming after him of Cromer's No.1 lifeboat by Admiral of the Fleet Sir John Cunningham. Mr Blogg, who retired last September, received from the Royal National Lifeboat Institution a portrait of himself, the work of Mr. T. C. Dugdale, RA, and a framed certificate of service. He also received a cheque and an illuminated address in a green morocco-covered album from many of his friends and admirers.' The ceremony was presided over by Viscount Templewood, president of the Cromer Branch, who said Blogg had become a national figure and the lifeboat station a great national institution. In receiving the lifeboat on behalf of the Branch, Blogg made what was the first public speech of his career: 'Thank you all very much. I am very pleased to accept this boat for the station, because I know it is the best boat that has ever been on it.' The service of dedication was conducted by the Reverend D. T. Dick, vicar of Cromer, and the Reverend W. Hughes, the Methodist minister. Coxswain Henry Davies presented his crew to Sir John, who said he was proud to name the boat after a very gallant man. 'I have much pleasure in naming her *Henry Blogg* and wish all who sail in her good luck on errands of mercy,' he declared. He then broke a bottle of wine on the lifeboat's stern and her launch was accompanied by cheers from the thousands ashore.

Henry Blogg at sea, possibly during trials. Although at 46ft she was of a standard length for the Watson cabin motor lifeboat, her deck layout was unusual in that she had two cabins. She was the first lifeboat to have a midship steering position and was sent to Cromer in the first place so that Coxswain Henry Blogg and his crew could test her out. (By courtesy of P. A. Vicary)

The reserve lifeboat *Edward Z. Dresden* arriving at Cromer from Grimsby on 3 April 1952, with 'Clacton-on-Sea Lifeboat' still adorning her stern. *Henry Blogg* had left earlier in the day to go to Rowhedge for overhaul and returned to Cromer on 12 July. (Photo supplied by Joyce Blyth)

Henry Blogg in the damaged boathouse following the major floods which hit the East Coast in January 1953. The boat was completely lifted off the slipway during the storm, as shown in the photo on the right, while the house itself suffered extensive damage. The pier was also badly damaged and was closed to the public until summer 1954.

Recovery of *Henry Blogg* with No.2 lifeboat *Harriot Dixon* passing the end of the slipway on lifeboat day, 11 August 1955. This photograph clearly shows the rudder and propeller arrangements on the 46ft Watson lifeboats, with the rudder recessed and the propellers protected by tunnels. (By courtesy of Eastern Counties Newspapers)

Henry Blogg towing the Sheringham lifeboat *Foresters' Centenary* on 31 May 1958 after the latter's engine had broken down. The service started at 9.50am when Cromer Coastguard informed the Sheringham honorary secretary that a request had been made by the Trinity House Superintendent at Great Yarmouth for the lifeboat to take a sick man off the Dudgeon Lightvessel. At 10.15am the Sheringham lifeboat *Foresters' Centenary* was launched with a doctor on board and reached the Lightvessel at 1.10pm. The doctor went aboard and gave the sick man a sedative, after which he was strapped to a stretcher and transferred to the lifeboat. The lifeboat then set off for her station but, at about 4.40pm, when nine miles north-east of Sheringham, the skew gear which drives the oil and water pumps broke down. *Henry Blogg* was therefore called out and took the Sheringham lifeboat in tow to her station, where both boats arrived at 7pm and the sick man was taken to hospital. The Cromer lifeboat returned to station at 7.40pm.

Henry Blogg launching down the slipway from the 1923 boathouse; the slipway caused a few problems with extensive maintenance work undertaken in 1924, 1947, 1950 and 1966. (From an old postcard supplied by Paul Russell)

Henry Blogg makes a spectacular sight as she launches on lifeboat day, 13 August 1953.
(By courtesy of Eastern Counties Newspapers)

Henry Blogg assisting the auxiliary yacht *Wima*, which had broken down and was drifting three miles off Trimingham. Second Coxswain Dick Davies was put on board the yacht, and secured a tow line, and the yacht was then towed to Great Yarmouth, 27 August 1958. (By courtesy of Joyce Blyth)

Two photographs of reserve lifeboat *Cunard* on duty during lifeboat day, 10 August 1961. The lifeboat was built in 1930 and served at St Mary's (Isles of Scilly) for twenty-five years. She undertook two services while at Cromer, the first on 2 February 1958, when she landed an injured man from the steamship *Hudson Bank*, of London. The second was on 2 March, when she went to the German motor vessel *Continental* and the British ship *Wansbeck*, which had been in collision ten miles north-west of the Haisborough Lightvessel. (Upper photo by courtesy of P. A. Vicary; lower photo by courtesy of Eastern Counties Newspapers)

Looking towards the lifeboat house and town with *Henry Blogg* launching down the slipway. This photograph shows how prominent a landmark the church was when seen from the sea. (By courtesy of P. A. Vicary)

The lifeboat crew pull a boy from his dinghy onto *Henry Blogg* in a flat clam sea. The 'rescue' was filmed on 9 August 1950, and shows David Tibble, nephew of Coxswain 'Shrimp' Davies, being taken on board the lifeboat. The footage was included in a film called 'Gale Warning' which was shown at Cromer's Regal Cinema on 11 August 1952. (Port of Lowestoft Research Society)

Henry Blogg alongside the motor vessel *Joika*, of Oslo, on 11 March 1964. The lifeboat launched to the Norwegian vessel, which had been in collision thirteen miles off Cromer. After standing by, the lifeboat crew decided that they should escort the vessel to Great Yarmouth.

Henry Blogg and No.2 lifeboat *Harriot Dixon* during an inspector's exercise, 11 April 1964. Before both boats launched they were inspected by six Icelandic MPs, who were spending a week in Britain visiting places connected with the fishing industry and the sea, including London, Norwich, Lowestoft, Hull and Cromer. (By courtesy of P. A. Vicary)

Edward and Isabella Irwin on lifeboat day, 5 August 1965. She arrived on 20 June, having travelled from Thorne, with an overnight stay in Wells. *Henry Blogg* had also left on 20 June for overhaul at Oulton Broad, from where she returned on 9 December, with the *Edward and Isabella Irwin* being left as reserve boat at Gorleston.

Henry Blogg at Gorleston in November 1965 with the Gorleston Coxswain George Mobbs standing on the quayside. She had just completed a refit and was waiting to go back to Cromer, but as the Gorleston lifeboat had been damaged on service on 24 November 1965, when she was searching for a missing boat named *Mandy*, the Cromer boat acted as a reserve lifeboat for a few days before returning to Cromer with *Edward and Isabella Irwin* coming in the opposite direction for relief duty at Gorleston. *Henry Blogg* had not gone straight back to Cromer after her refit because the weather was too bad for rehousing. (By courtesy of Eastern Counties Newspapers)

Henry Blogg at moorings during a spell of reserve duty, possibly at Appledore. (By courtesy of the RNLI)

Oil rig Sea Gem

During the last days of 1965, *Henry Blogg* and lifeboats from neighbouring stations were involved in the search for survivors from the oil rig *Sea Gem*, which sank in the North Sea on 27 December with thirty-two crew on board. Five of the crew died in the disaster, nineteen were saved by the steamship *Baltrover* and eight men were unaccounted for. The oil rig was forty-seven miles north-west of Cromer and thirty-six miles north-east of Spurn Point.

Lifeboats from Humber, Cromer, Skegness and Wells were called out to search for the survivors and spent a total of 113 hours at sea, but were unable to find anyone. The first lifeboat to be launched was *City of Bradford III* from the Humber, which put out at 2.40pm and arrived at the scene five hours later. She carried out an extensive search of the area in conjunction with aircraft and other vessels and returned to her station at 4.25am on 29 December, having been at sea for nearly thirty-eight hours.

Skegness lifeboat *Charles Fred Grantham* was launched at 6.30am on 28 December and carried out a search north-north-east to the Dowsing Lightvessel, and then to the position of the casualty. She returned past the Humber Lightvessel down the coast to Skegness and returned to her station after fourteen hours at sea. Cromer lifeboat *Henry Blogg* launched at 10.40am on 28 December and searched the area of the casualty as well as standing by while salvage operations were attempted. After twenty-seven hours at sea, she returned to her station to be relieved by Wells lifeboat *Ernest Tom Neathercoat,* which also stood by during salvage operations and was on service for twenty-one hours.

On 30 December, the Humber lifeboat again launched to take a party of divers to the wreck, and she also helped with salvage operations. These combined searches were carried out in northerly winds of up to gale force, accompanied by a very heavy swell with sleet and rain falling intermittently throughout. In recognition of the lifeboats' assistance, the British Petroleum Co made a donation to the crews.

The crew of *Henry Blogg* following the service to the oil rig *Sea Gem*, December 1965. Pictured left to right are: Dick Davies (coxswain for the service), John Allen (mechanic), Billy Davies, Brian Lee, 'Stymie' Blyth, Richard Davies, 'Yacker' Harrison, Paddy Vaughan, John Balls, John'o Lee and 'Kelly' Harrison. (Photo supplied by Joyce Blyth)

Henry Blogg returning from service to the oil rig *Sea Gem* on 29 December 1965 after what was one of her final services before she left the station. (By courtesy of Eastern Counties Newspapers)

1923-67 • No.2 lifeboats

The No.2 station at Cromer was operational from 1923, when the new pier boathouse was completed, until 1967. With the arrival of the motor lifeboat which was slipway launched, *Louisa Heartwell* was designated as the No.2 lifeboat and she remained in this role until being replaced by another sailing craft. The need for two lifeboats at Cromer was explained in local newspaper reports: 'It is imperative that when the present motor boat is away on service, having regard to the mileage she has to protect for life-saving purposes, that a second boat should be in readiness.'

On 22 May 1931, the 'new' lifeboat, *Alexandra*, arrived to serve at the No.2 station. She was towed from Great Yarmouth by *H. F. Bailey* and was successfully housed in the East Gangway boathouse on a new carriage. The new boat was a Liverpool type similar to *Louisa Heartwell*, 36ft in length, pulling twelve oars and previously stationed at Hope Cove, in South Devon. Whether a pulling lifeboat was needed at this time is open to question as *Alexandra* did not perform any effective rescues, although she did launch three times, without success, to the barge *Sepoy* on 13 December 1933. She remained at Cromer until July 1934, when she was sold out of service.

The beach-launched boat was retained because, in certain states of weather, recovering the motor lifeboat up the slipway was impossible, and so she would go to Gorleston to shelter until conditions improved. At these times, cover was provided by the No.2 lifeboat, the importance of which is reflected by the stationing of a second motor lifeboat at Cromer in 1934.

The new No.2 lifeboat was a 35ft 6in Liverpool class motor lifeboat, *Harriot Dixon*. She was built by Groves & Guttridge, at Cowes, and arrived at Cromer on 4 August after a passage from her builder's via Ramsgate and Gorleston. Commander Vaux, the Lifeboat Inspector, accompanied Coxswain Blogg and his crew on the trip. *Harriot Dixon* served as the No.2 lifeboat for thirty years and performed a number of useful services, many in conjunction with or backing up the No.1 lifeboat.

She was replaced in 1967 by the 37ft Oakley *William Henry and Mary King*, which was the last No.2 lifeboat to serve at Cromer. The Oakley was self-righting by virtue of a water ballast righting system and was the first self-righting lifeboat to serve at Cromer in the twentieth century. Built by J. S. White, she was fitted with twin 52hp Parsons Porbeagle diesel engines. She was placed on station in October 1964 and, during her time at Cromer, launched twelve times on service and saved one life. She was subsequently transferred to the Bridlington station in Yorkshire.

In place of *Louisa Heartwell*, the 1903-built lifeboat *Alexandra* was supplied as the beach-launched No.2 lifeboat. She only served for three years and is seen here launching for lifeboat day, watched by a large crowd of onlookers. (From an old photo supplied by Paul Russell)

The No.2 lifeboat *Alexandra* is prepared for launching on lifeboat day, August 1931. *Alexandra* came to Cromer in May 1931 as an interim measure after *Louisa Heartwell* had been found to be faulty and in need of replacing. Built in 1903 by Thames Iron Works, *Alexandra* was a 35ft Liverpool type and served at Hope Cove in Devon from August 1903 to May 1930, saving two lives and launching on service eighteen times. She served at Cromer for just over three years, leaving in July 1934 as the last pulling and sailing lifeboat to be operated from the station. She launched only three times while at Cromer, and was sold out of service a few days after being replaced.

Harriot Dixon slides off the carriage and into the water, with the launchers pulling on the launching ropes to get the boat afloat. The 35ft 6in Liverpool was light enough to be manhandled across the beach and many boats of the design were built for stations which practised carriage launching, including Cromer's neighbouring station of Sheringham. (By courtesy of P. A. Vicary)

(Right) *Harriot Dixon* is launched by motorised tractor. No fewer than five different tractors were at the station during this lifeboat's thirty-year career at Cromer.

Harriot Dixon outside the lifeboat house on the gangway with tractor T49, the fourth tractor to serve at Cromer, on station from 1949 until 1960, and also the station's longest-serving launch vehicle. (From an old postcard supplied by Paul Russell)

No.2 lifeboat *Harriot Dixon* at sea with Coxswain Henry Blogg at the wheel. Blogg was Superintendent Coxswain of both boats until his retirement in 1947, when separate coxswains were appointed, one for each boat. (From a postcard supplied by Paul Russell)

Harriot Dixon is launched for a lifeboat day demonstration, 4 August 1935. She was funded from the legacy of £3,750 left by the late William Edward Dixon, a surgeon, of West Worthing, Sussex. He had died in 1921 and left the money for a lifeboat to be named after his mother and stationed, if possible, on the Kent or East coast. (By courtesy of P. A. Vicary)

Harriot Dixon on the beach with crew; pictured, left to right, are: L. J. Harrison (jnr), Joe Linder, George Cox, Henry 'Shrimp' Davies, W. H. Davies, J. W. Davies, J. J. Davies (snr), L. J. Harrison (snr), W. T. Davies, Coxswain Henry Blogg, Tom 'Bussey' Allen, Bob 'Skinback' Cox, Arthur Balls, Walter Burgess, George 'Buckram' Balls and 'Lantern Bob' Davies. (From an old postcard supplied by Paul Russell)

Harriot Dixon at sea off the pier with Coxswain Jimmy Davies at the helm. With her arrival as the No.2 lifeboat, Cromer become one of only a handful of stations that operated two motor lifeboats at the same time. (By courtesy of Port of Lowestoft Research Society)

Harriot Dixon being recovered on the East Beach on the morning of Sunday 31 May 1953. She is landing eleven councillors and prominent local people who, the evening before, had visited HMS *Cheerful*, which was on a five-day courtesy visit to Cromer. The weather had prevented them from being landed at the pier on the previous night, and so the lifeboat went out to collect them. Although that service in itself was uneventful, it was significant as, five days later, three of the lifeboat crew involved were drowned in a tragedy which befell the fishing boat *Boy Jimmy*. They were Coxswain Jimmy Davies, his brother, the second mechanic Frank Davies, and twenty-one-year-old Ted Bussey.

No.2 lifeboat *Harriot Dixon* being launched by tractor T49 from the East Gangway boathouse, watched by a large crowd on lifeboat day, 11 August 1955.

Recovery of *Harriot Dixon* on the beach; the hauling chain can be seen attached to the keel at the bow.

A dramatic photograph of *Harriot Dixon* putting off through the surf and heading for Oulton Broad to go to a boatyard there for some minor modifications, 4 July 1962. (By courtesy of Joyce Blyth)

No.2 lifeboat *Harriot Dixon* being launched across the beach by tractor T49, registration number KGP 854. The tractor was supplied to the station during the 1930s to make launching the No.2 lifeboat easier.

RAF Whirlwind helicopter from Horsham St Faith approaching *Harriot Dixon*. On board the lifeboat are, from left to right, Eddie Marsh, 'Tuna' Harrison, Paddy Vaughan, David Leeder and Chris Craske, on lifeboat day, 7 August 1962. (Photo by courtesy of David Leeder)

Reserve 35ft 6in Liverpool *Jose Neville* at the East Gangway on her arrival at Cromer, 15 June 1964. She served from 15 June until 9 September 1964, launching once on service.

Jose Neville launching on lifeboat day, 13 August 1964. (Photo by courtesy of David Leeder)

The new No.2 lifeboat, 37ft Oakley *William Henry and Mary King*, arrives at Cromer for the first time, 24 October 1964, after passage from Cowes. Her passage from her builder's on the Isle of Wight to her new station was described in *The Lifeboat* for March 1965 in an article 'On passage with the RNLI' by the station's honorary secretary, Dr P. S. Barclay. (By courtesy of Eastern Counties Newspapers)

No.2 lifeboat *William Henry and Mary King* returning to the beach, following an exercise, with the new Case 1000D tractor T78 (registration BYN 568B), a more powerful vehicle than her predecessors, sent to the station to assist with the launch and recovery of the new 37ft Oakley lifeboat. (By courtesy of Ted Luckin)

In front of a large crowd on a blustery summer day, *William Henry and Mary King* is launched at the end of her naming ceremony, 8 July 1965. Christened by Princess Marina, she was funded from the legacy of Miss Jane Graham King, of Surrey, in memory of her father and mother. (By courtesy of Eastern Counties Newspapers)

(Right) Princess Marina at the naming ceremony of *William Henry and Mary King* with, from left to right, David Leeder, John Lee, George Lusher, Peter Grout, Richard Davies and Henry 'Shrimp' Davies.

William Henry and Mary King was launched on 1 July 1966 to stand by the fishing vessel *Universal Dipper,* which had run aground in fog at East Runton. When *Universal Dipper* was refloated, *William Henry and Mary King* escorted her safely to Great Yarmouth.

1967–84 • Ruby and Arthur Reed

In 1967, the latest offshore lifeboat to serve at Cromer was placed on station. The boat was funded by Mrs R. M. Reed, of Eastbourne, whose gift was made in memory of her husband, Mr A. E. Reed, of Stamford, and was named *Ruby and Arthur Reed*. Alterations were made to the pier boathouse prior to the new lifeboat's arrival, which was of the 48ft 6in Oakley class, a wooden-hulled self-righting design. Her displacement of thirty tons included almost three tons of water ballast which was used in the unusual self-righting mechanism. The wheelhouse was positioned amidships and was fully enclosed to provide crew protection, with an aft cabin serving as a chartroom and housing for the electronic equipment.

The new lifeboat was ready for service by March 1967 and, after extended sea trials, set off for her station. She reached Cromer Pier at noon on 11 March 1967 to be housed for the first time. Although a rough sea and freshening wind suggested that a practice launch would not be possible, the weather improved and a launch was undertaken. At some point during this first exercise, either when the lifeboat ran down the slipway or when she was being rehoused, the port propeller was damaged and about six feet of the oak bilge keel on the port side was splintered. Although the damage was not as bad as at first feared, the boat was taken away and went to Lowestoft for repairs, leaving the No.2 lifeboat to stand in, while modifications were made to the slipway.

During the seventeen years she served at Cromer, *Ruby and Arthur Reed* launched on service 125 times and saved fifty-eight lives. In September 1984 she left the station for the last time, went to Fletcher's Boatyard at Lowestoft for survey and overhaul and was reallocated to St David's in Pembrokeshire. She served the Welsh station for two and a half years, saving nine lives during that time, and was then sold out of service during September 1988, without engines. She is now on display at Hythe Village Marina, near Southampton, out of the water in the car park.

An excellent photograph of 48ft 6in Oakley *Ruby and Arthur Reed* at speed off Cromer pier, March 1967. (By courtesy of Maritime Photo Library)

Ruby and Arthur Reed arriving at Gorleston on passage to her station, 13 March 1967. She had been completed in 1966 at Littlehampton by William Osborne Ltd and was fitted with twin 110hp Gardner 6LX six-cylinder diesel engines which gave a speed of approximately nine knots. She was a 48ft 6in Oakley wooden-hulled self-righter with a displacement of thirty tons that included almost three tons of water ballast. During her passage to Cromer, before she had reached her destination, she had performed her first service. As she sailed past Overstrand, the passage crew on board spotted one of the Cox brothers broken down offshore in his fishing boat. Although he was in no danger, the lifeboat gave him a helping tow along to Cromer where he rowed ashore. (By courtesy of Eastern Counties Newspapers Ltd)

Ruby and Arthur Reed undergoing her self-righting trials. Unusually, she had two self-righting trials, both at Portsmouth in June 1966. The trial involved turning the boat through 180 degrees and then she righted herself in six seconds. The first took place on 22 June, with the second the following day for the benefit of the media and her donor, Mrs R. M. Reed.

Ruby and Arthur Reed off the pier for the first time, at noon on 14 March 1967. Before she reached Cromer, the new lifeboat had performed her first service, as described on the previous page. The new lifeboat was housed for the first time with great care. Although a rough sea and freshening wind suggested that a practice launch would not be possible, the weather improved and a launch was undertaken. At some point during this first exercise, either when the lifeboat ran down the slipway or when she was being rehoused, the port propeller was damaged and about six feet of the oak bilge keel on the port side was splintered. The boat was taken to Lowestoft for repairs, while modifications were effected to the slipway. Once these were finished, she returned to station to begin her service career. During the temporary absence of the new boat, No.2 lifeboat *William Henry and Mary King*, to be withdrawn once the new lifeboat was operational, covered the area. (By courtesy of Maritime Photo Library and Eastern Counties Newspapers Ltd)

Ruby and Arthur Reed on the slipway prior to her naming ceremony on 21 June 1967. The donor, Mrs Ruby Reed, was on hand to christen the boat in memory of herself and her husband, Mr A. E. Reed, of Stamford in Lincolnshire. She was presented to the crew by Coxswain Henry 'Shrimp' Davies before the formal dedication. During the ceremony, the service of dedication was conducted by the Right Reverend The Lord Bishop of Lynn, Rt Rev W. S. Llewellyn, MA, assisted by Rev C. W. J. Searle-Barnes, MA, Vicar of Cromer and Rev J. R. Sharp, Minister of Cromer Methodist Church. (By courtesy of Eastern Counties Newspapers Ltd)

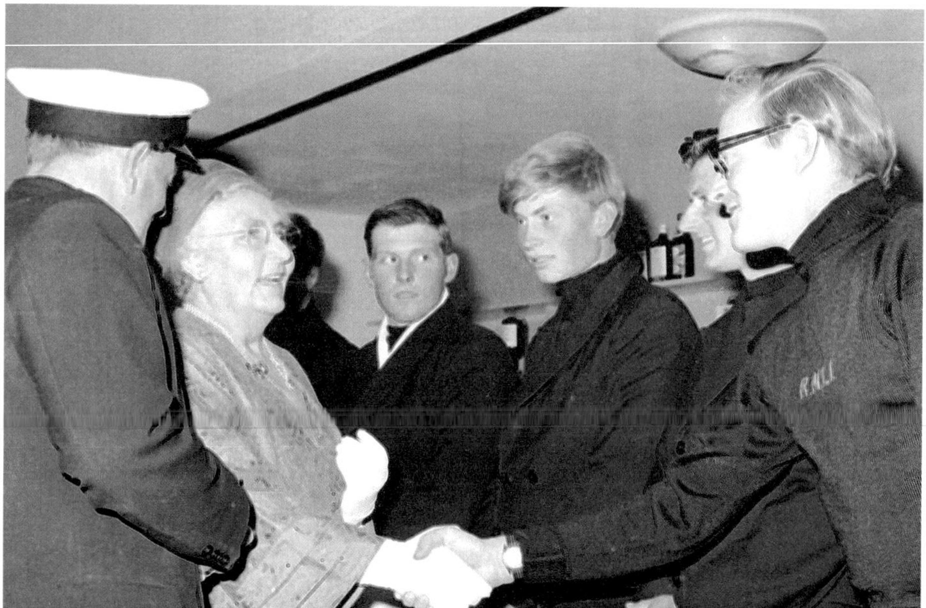

(Left) 'Shrimp' Davies, Mrs Ruby Reed, Richard Davies, Billy Davies, David Leeder and Paddy Vaughan following the naming.

Ruby and Arthur Reed being launched at the end of her naming ceremony (above) for a short demonstration at sea. In attendance at the ceremony were lifeboats from the neighbouring stations of Caister and Sheringham. The photograph below shows *Ruby and Arthur Reed* at sea with Sheringham lifeboat *Manchester Unity of Oddfellows*, a 37ft Oakley lifeboat that served Cromer's neighbouring station until 1990. (By courtesy of Eastern Counties Newspapers Ltd)

A spectacular photograph of *Ruby and Arthur Reed* launching in heavy swell. (By courtesy of P. A. Vicary)

Ruby and Arthur Reed returning from a routine service to a dinghy on 4 February 1968, from which she saved three people. (By courtesy of Eastern Counties Newspapers Ltd)

Ruby and Arthur Reed landing an injured man from the motor launch *Pinnace* on 2 March 1968. The lifeboat had launched in the late afternoon after the coxswain and mechanic had seen distress flares from a small vessel two miles north-west of the lifeboat house. The casualty was found bumping on rocks and being driven towards the shore by a light north-easterly breeze, so *Ruby and Arthur Reed* towed it to deeper water where it was found that one of her crew of two had an injured finger. He was taken aboard the lifeboat, while three of the lifeboat's crew went aboard the vessel to help anchor her. The injured man was taken to Cromer for hospital treatment, after which the lifeboat returned to the casualty and took the launch in tow to Blakeney. A local boat acted as a pilot boat to the lifeboat and the casualty was towed safely to Blakeney Pit. Owing to poor visibility and a freshening wind, the coxswain decided to leave the lifeboat at Blakeney overnight, and she returned to station to be rehoused on 3 March. (By courtesy of Eastern Counties Newspapers Ltd)

(Right) *Ruby and Arthur Reed* at William Osborne's yard at Littlehampton for her first major refit, July 1973. (Jeff Morris)

Reserve lifeboat *The Good Hope* (ON.821) exercising with D-197 and a Whirlwind helicopter from RAF Coltishall during the lifeboat day display on Thursday 9 August 1973. A 46ft Watson motor built in 1939, *The Good Hope* was stationed at Montrose until 1972 and then served in the Reserve (later Relief) Fleet until 1981. She was at Cromer from June 1973 until 20 March 1974, during which time she saved four lives and was involved in the medal-winning service to the deep-sea trawler *Boston Jaguar*.

(Left) Reserve lifeboat *The Good Hope* arriving at Gorleston on 30 November 1973 following the service to the fishing vessel *Katrina Ann* R.91, during which she saved the lives of the four crew. (By courtesy of Eastern Counties Newspapers Ltd)

The crew of the lifeboat involved in the service to the trawler *Boston Jaguar*. Dr Paul Barclay was awarded the Bronze medal; the Thanks of the Institution inscribed on Vellum was accorded to Coxswain Henry Davies and crew member Richard Davies. Medal service certificates were presented to the remainder of the crew, Second Coxswain Lewis 'Tuna' Harrison, Mechanic R. Amey, Assistant Mechanic Leslie 'Yacker' Harrison, and crew members John Lee and W. H. Davies. The awards were presented on 8 August 1974 and, with the RNLI's Thanks Inscribed on Vellum, are, left to right, Ralph Amey, William Davies, Richard Davies, Lewis Harrison, Coxswain Henry 'Shrimp' Davies, John Lee, L. J. Harrison, Dr Paul Barclay and Wing Commander Clive Sinton. (By courtesy of Eastern Counties Newspapers Ltd)

Boston Jaguar

On 15 November 1973, an explosion aboard the 300-ton deep-sea trawler *Boston Jaguar* left the ship without steering gear, the mate killed and a crew member injured. She was thirty-seven miles from Cromer and the injured man needed to be taken ashore as soon as possible. As medical help was needed, local GP Dr Paul Barclay decided that, although prone to seasickness, he must go. So, at 11.10pm, the reserve lifeboat *The Good Hope* launched into north-westerly gale force winds with Dr Barclay aboard.

The trawler *Boston Wasp* had taken *Boston Jaguar* in tow and headed for the Dudgeon lightvessel. The lifeboat established radio contact with both trawlers and reached the lightvessel at 1.30am, travelling twenty-one miles in two hours and twenty minutes. An hour later, the lifeboat reached the casualty and Coxswain Davies took the lifeboat alongside *Boston Jaguar* to pass a securing line. At the third attempt to get the lifeboat alongside the trawler the coxswain was able to hold the lifeboat alongside long enough to allow Dr Barclay and crewman Richard Davies to jump across onto the trawler.

Once aboard, Dr Barclay found the mate of the trawler was dead, and, with help from Davies, attended to the injured deckhand who had facial lacerations and was severely shocked. As Coxswain Davies considered it imprudent to attempt to go alongside *Boston Jaguar* a second time, Dr Barclay and Richard Davies remained aboard despite the doctor suffering from severe seasickness. Davies helped to maintain the vessel's course during the tow and at 6am the vessels arrived off Cromer.

With the lifeboat standing by, at first light a helicopter from RAF Coltishall lifted off the injured deckhand and Dr Barclay, and took them to Cromer Hospital to be assessed. Due to the rough sea conditions, rehousing was impossible and so the lifeboat, after Richard Davies had been transferred back on board, made for Great Yarmouth, in company with the tow to await a change in the weather.

Ruby and Arthur Reed launches with reserve lifeboat *The Good Hope* standing by off the pier, 20 March 1974. (By courtesy of Eastern Counties Newspapers Ltd)

Ruby and Arthur Reed returning from service to the cargo vessel *Atlantic Duke*, which went aground near the South Middle Haisborough Buoy on 19 February 1977. Another cargo vessel, *American Moon*, was standing by as *Ruby and Arthur Reed* launched at 9.27am. The lifeboat reached the casualty an hour and a half later to relieve the Gorleston lifeboat, which had been on the scene throughout the night. The casualty was eventually refloated at 10.48am on 20 February, and the Cromer lifeboat left the scene at 11.50am, returning to station just over two hours later. (By courtesy of Eastern Counties Newspapers Ltd)

Ruby and Arthur Reed towing the catamaran *Katabatic* back to Cromer pier after it had capsized, 22 February 1977. The lifeboat towed the casualty to the mooring buoy, from where it was recovered by the owner, while the survivors were landed at the boathouse.

Ruby and Arthur Reed entering Gorleston harbour with the captain of the capsized cargo vessel *Nimrod*, in November 1977, after a long and difficult service in heavy seas. (By courtesy of Eastern Counties Newspapers Ltd)

Mechanic Ralph Amey inspects the damage to the boathouse doors caused by storms, January 1978. The exposed position of the boathouse at the end of Cromer pier made it susceptible to storm damage, and on several occasions it was damaged by the full force of the North Sea. (By courtesy of Eastern Counties Newspapers Ltd)

Relief lifeboat *William Gammon - Manchester & District XXX* (ON. 849) launching in rough weather on 30 December 1978 to go to the aid of the listing motor vessel *Diana V* of Rotterdam. The distressed vessel was able to increase speed and made for the Humber, so after nine miles the Cromer lifeboat was recalled. Nearing the Humber, the motor vessel broke down again and the Humber lifeboat *City of Bradford IV* (ON.1052) went to her aid, a rescue which earned her Coxswain Brian Bevan the Silver medal. The Cromer crew were forced to take shelter in Great Yarmouth harbour and, although not directly involved in the rescue, the launch and subsequent passage had been a severe test of boat and crew. (Poppyland Photos)

Relief 46ft 9in Watson lifeboat *William Gammon - Manchester and District XXX* (ON.849), built in 1947 and originally stationed at The Mumbles, was on station while *Ruby and Arthur Reed* went for refit during 1978 to 1979, and performed only one effective service during her time at Cromer, on 6 March 1979, from which she is pictured returning. After a crewman on board the Haisborough Lightvessel had fallen down a ladder and injured his back and legs, requiring medical assistance, the lifeboat launched at 1.35pm with the station's Honorary Medical Adviser on board and reached the Lightvessel at 3.10pm. The doctor, coxswain and three crew then went aboard, and first aid and morphine were administered by the doctor. Due to the man's injured back, considerable care had to be exercised in moving him but he was taken onto the lifeboat, which left the Lightvessel at 4pm and arrived at station just over an hour later. The lifeboat was rehoused and the casualty passed to waiting ambulance men, who took him to the Norfolk and Norwich Hospital. (By courtesy of Eastern Counties Newspapers Ltd)

Ruby and Arthur Reed landing a liferaft from the cargo vessel *Ems* on 30 January 1981, to which she launched on service at 1.05am after reports of a collision between two ships near the Mid Haisborough Buoy. The lifeboat arrived on the scene at 2.20am to find the cargo vessel had sunk after being in collision with a smaller vessel, *Udine*, which with other ships in the area had rescued twenty-one people although two were still missing. *Udine* was acting as on-scene commander while the area was combed for the missing men, with both Cromer and Gorleston lifeboats assisting in the search through the debris, containers and upturned liferafts over a large area and in thick fog. At daybreak, Cromer lifeboat found two upturned liferafts still attached to the sunken vessel, so these were checked then left to mark the wreck. The search was abandoned at 9.35am and *Ruby and Arthur Reed* returned to station at 11am with a liferaft.

The lifeboat crew after the service to the cargo vessel *Ems*, January 1981, from left to right: Coxswain Richard Davies, Clive Rayment, Dick West, Billy Davies, Mac MacKinnon, Donny Abbs and John Jonas. (Both photos by courtesy of Eastern Counties Newspapers Ltd)

Ruby and Arthur Reed and the crab boat *Provider* off the beach, 2 June 1981. What proved to be the last service performed by *Ruby and Arthur Reed* at Cromer took place on 4 September 1984 when she went to *Provider*, and another crab boat, *Star*, which had been working between Mundesley and Bacton. (By courtesy of Eastern Counties Newspapers)

Ruby and Arthur Reed arriving at Great Yarmouth following the service to the oil rig supply vessel *The Cuttlefish* on 30 November 1981. The supply vessel had grounded on the Haisborough Sands in rough seas and four men were taken off by helicopter. Two others were taken off by the lifeboat, which touched the bottom going across the sandbank but got clear safely. She left the casualty at 6.30pm and arrived at Great Yarmouth two hours later, where she was forced to remain until 3 December, when the weather abated and rehousing was possible. (By courtesy of Eastern Counties Newspapers Ltd)

Ruby and Arthur Reed with the 37ft Oakley relief lifeboat *Calouste Gulbenkian* from Sheringham and an RAF Wessex air-sea rescue helicopter on lifeboat day, 12 August 1982. (Paul Russell)

Ruby and Arthur Reed with the station's inshore lifeboat, D-307 *Spirit of Round Table*, following the dedication of the new ILB boathouse on the East Beach, 19 August 1984. (Paul Russell)

Ruby and Arthur Reed launching on 19 August 1984, her last exercise launch before she left Cromer. Her next launch was on service to the *Provider*, on 4 September, after which she went to Great Yarmouth due to the weather conditions, and never returned to Cromer. (Paul Russell)

Ruby and Arthur Reed at sea for lifeboat day, August 1984, undertaking a mock rescue involving a small sailing dinghy. After leaving service, *Ruby and Arthur Reed* was transferred to St David's in South Wales in 1985, where she served until 1988. She was sold out of service in September 1988, without engines, for display as a static exhibit at Hythe Village Marina, Southampton Water, in the middle of a roundabout. (Nicholas Leach)

Following her departure from Cromer in September 1984, *Ruby and Arthur Reed* was taken to Fletcher's yard, Oulton Broad, where she was refitted in preparation for service at St David's, April 1985. (Frank Muirhead).

Inshore lifeboats

The inshore rescue boat (IRB) was a new type of rescue craft intended to answer the type of calls that were increasingly being made on lifeboats not just at Cromer but at stations throughout the British Isles. As a result of growing numbers of people using the sea for recreational activities during the 1960s, inshore incidents which lifeboats went to had risen dramatically. Conventional offshore lifeboats, such as *Henry Blogg*, were not well suited to such work and a simple, fast rescue craft was required. IRBs, later known as inshore lifeboats (ILB), were introduced into Britain in 1963, since when the design has been refined and developed, and the small boats have become ever more efficient and effective life-saving tools.

The ILB's advantage over the conventional lifeboat was its speed which, at twenty knots, was considerably faster than any lifeboat in service during the 1960s. The decision to place an ILB at Cromer was made on 15 February 1967 when a meeting was held to discuss the placing of an ILB at the station, and ten volunteers put their names forward as crew members. The first boat, No.101, arrived on 15 March and two days later was exercised in heavy surf conditions under Divisional Inspector Dag Pike. The boat was subsequently placed on station, thus maintaining the tradition of two lifeboats at Cromer, but had to wait until 6 June for its first call.

Since 1967, several inshore lifeboats have served the station, getting progressively more advanced and sophisticated. During the 1970s, D-197, funded by the Gravesend Branch, was on station and was replaced in 1984 by D-307 *Spirit of Round Table*. This, in turn, was replaced by D-436 *Chloe* in 1992. The station's latest inshore lifeboat, D-568 *Seahorse III*, was declared operational on 20 June 2001 and the ILBs remain an integral part of the lifeboat station.

The 16ft ILBs, such as No.101 pictured here, were made from nylon coated with hypalon, crewed by two or three, powered by a 40hp outboard engine, and launched quickly and easily using a trolley across the beach. Pictured are, left to right, Donny Abbs (hidden), Inspector Dag Pike, Ted Luckin and Alastair Mayes.

Inshore lifeboat D-101 pictured in March 1967 on her arrival at the station. She effectively took the place of the No.2 lifeboat. The first ILB arrived in March 1967, four years after the RNLI's first ILB had entered service. (By courtesy of Eastern Counties Newspapers Ltd)

Cromer's first inshore lifeboat, D-101, pictured two days after her arrival and about to be put through her paces off the beach. (By courtesy of Eastern Counties Newspapers Ltd)

D-101 returns to the beach after rescuing two bathers in difficulty, 2 July 1968. For this kind of rescue, where speed was essential, the inflatable ILB was an ideal craft. (By courtesy of Eastern Counties Newspapers Ltd)

The second ILB to serve at the station, D-26, outside the ILB house, August 1970. The ILB was initially based at the East Gangway boathouse and housed in the 1902 lifeboat house. However, in August 1970 it was moved to this boathouse, located to the west of the pier at the foot of the Melbourne slope. Built from glass fibre, the house became known as the 'igloo' because of its appearance. Moving to this location was intended to overcome the problem of being blocked by fishing boats drawn up in front of the East Gangway. Pictured are, left to right: Alistair Mayes, Richard Hack, Tony Spurgeon, John Wells, Eric Love, Ted Luckin, Donny Abbs and Geoff Morris. (By courtesy of Ted Luckin)

D-26 lands four survivors from an inflatable dinghy, 19 July 1971. The ILB had gone to the aid of the dinghy, which had capsized about half-a-mile off the east beach. The dinghy's four occupants, all wearing life jackets, were in the water so were picked up and brought back to the beach. This was one of fourteen service launches completed by the ILB during the year, during which five lives were saved. Theo Stibbons is pictured, centre, carrying one of the rescued children to safety. (By courtesy of Eastern Counties Newspapers Ltd)

Crew members with the inshore lifeboat D-197, from left to right: David Durrant, Alistair Mayes, Frank Muirhead, Ted Luckin, Neil MacKinnon, Eric Love, Donny Abbs and John Andrews. (By courtesy of Ted Luckin)

D class inflatable D-197 on her trolley outside the lifeboat museum with, from left to right, Don Harvey, Donny Abbs and Honorary Secretary Jim Smith, pictured in April 1979 when conditions made launching across the West Beach impossible, so the ILB was temporarily kept in the museum. (By courtesy of Eastern Counties Newspapers Ltd)

The third ILB to serve at Cromer was D-197, funded by the Gravesend Branch, at sea with crew David Durrant on board, and Ted Luckin at the helm. (By courtesy of Ted Luckin)

D class inflatable D-197 on exercise, with Theo Stibbons at the helm, Peter Stibbons on the right and Ted Luckin also on board. (By courtesy of Ted Luckin)

A dramatic photograph of D-197 being launched through the surf off the beach, with Donny Abbs on the helm. The conditions for launching off the beach can often be difficult and dangerous for both lifeboat crew and shore helpers. (By courtesy of Eastern Counties Newspapers Ltd)

D-197 alongside the pier, 12 September 1972, during the service by the offshore lifeboat to the cabin cruiser *New Prince of Wales*, which requested assistance after taking water into her engine room. (By courtesy of Eastern Counties Newspapers Ltd)

Relief inshore lifeboat D-96 assisting the 43ft motor launch *Enterprise*, 11 June 1979. The motor launch was seen in difficulty off Sheringham and so the ILB was launched at 3.07pm to her aid. The ILB reached the vessel at 3.12pm and towed it into deeper water to the west of the pier. (By courtesy of Eastern Counties Newspapers Ltd)

D-197 exercising with a Whirlwind Mk.10 RAF rescue helicopter.

Chris Craske, Helmsman Clive Rayment and Frank Muirhead, pictured outside the East Gangway lifeboat house, were involved in one of the most outstanding rescues in which the ILB has been involved. The Bronze medal was awarded to Helmsman Rayment and medal service certificates were presented to the two crew. (By courtesy of Eastern Counties Newspapers Ltd)

George William

At lunchtime on 1 May 1981, the ILB was launched to the crab boat *George William*, which had sunk off East Runton, with the boat's two crew being thrown into the water. Within six minutes of the call, the ILB was at sea, with good visibility but a fresh to strong force five to six breeze, creating a moderate to rough sea. As the ILB went through the surf off the beach, although the outboard engine was tilted to clear the ground, the propeller touched bottom in the troughs.

Once clear of the surf, a course was set for the casualty, a mile and a half to the west. Maximum speed was maintained as far as possible, but the engine had to be eased back to get the craft through the bigger seas. As she neared the casualty, the ILB crew was informed that the two fishermen were in the water 150 yards off East Runton beach. An approach was made from the north through seas breaking in shallows over an offshore bank. The lifeboat then had to round the capsized crab boat and floating debris to reach the men in the water. One fisherman was hanging on to a lifebuoy, the other to a crab pot marker buoy and, by 12.30pm, both were safely aboard the ILB.

The survivors were suffering from hypothermia, but landing at East Runton was too risky as conditions had deteriorated, and the onshore sea and swell had increased. So the ILB was taken as fast as possible to Cromer, with the crew members tending to the survivors. At 12.37pm, the ILB was beached at Cromer, where the two survivors were carried to a waiting ambulance. For this difficult service, the Bronze medal was awarded to Helmsman Rayment and medal service certificates went to the crew members.

D-211 outside the ILB house in 1983. The unusual 'igloo' building was used to house the ILB from 1970 to 1984. (Paul Russell)

D-307 *Spirit of Round Table* at speed on lifeboat day, 6 August 1992, with David Pope on the helm. She was on station from 1984 until 1992, launching on service a total of eighty-one times and saving thirty lives. (Paul Russell)

The ILB house on the East Beach used for housing the D class inflatables from 1984 until 2004. The building was dismantled in 2005 to make way for the new Lifeboat Museum. D class inflatable D-307 can be seen on her trolley inside the house. (Nicholas Leach)

In August 1992, a new D class inflatable, D-436 *Chloe*, was placed on station. The station's fifth ILB, she was funded from the gift of Miss Iris Buckle, of Hertfordshire, in memory of her mother, Chloe Long, of Hemsby, and was named on 11 July 1993 at a ceremony held on the seafront outside the ILB house. After the ceremony, Senior Helmsman David Pope and two crew members took the boat to sea for a demonstration alongside the all-weather lifeboat. (Paul Russell)

Launching D-436 *Chloe* for lifeboat day, 8 August 1996. The tractor was provided to make launching and recovery faster and safer. D-436 served at Cromer until 2001, launching on service more than fifty times. (Paul Russell)

D-436 *Chloe* launching across the East Beach using tractor TA34, June 1998. D-436 was one of the 16ft 3in Avon EA16 type ILBs, developed by the RNLI to improve upon previous designs of inflatable lifeboat. After being pushed across the beach, the ILB is manhandled on her trolley into the water to be launched. (Nicholas Leach)

Relief D class inflatable D-419 *Sarah Helena* being recovered by tractor TA34 on 1 November 1998. She served at Cromer twice, in 1997 and 1998, launching on service a total of ten times. (Paul Russell)

A number of relief D class inflatables have sevred the station, including D-465 *Palmer Bayer*, which was on station in 2002 and launched four times on service. (Paul Russell)

Relief D class inflatable D-441 *Irish Diver* on exercise, 19 October 2003. On board are Adam Lincoln (helm), Rob Jackson and Mearl Brown. D-441 served from September 2003 to January 2004. Built in 1993, D-441 served at Dun Laoghaire until 2001, then Trearddur Bay, and was placed in the Relief Fleet in 2002. (Paul Russell)

Relief D class inflatable D-439 *Phyllis Mary* in the surf. She served during 2000 and launched five times. (Paul Russell)

Relief D class inflatable D-485 *Stafford with Rugeley* launching on exercise in October 2005; she served from June to October 2005, and launched on service twelve times. (Paul Russell)

Relief D class inflatable D-433 *Marjorie* launching on exercise, 7 March 1999. (Paul Russell)

The scene outside the Lifeboat Museum on 20 October 2002 during the naming and dedication ceremony of D-568 *Seahorse III*, with Station Admin Officer Peter Stibbons giving a reading. At the end of the ceremony, the new boat was christened by Mrs Barbara New. (Paul Russell)

D-568 *Seahorse III* being put through her paces off the beach after her naming ceremony, 20 October 2002, with Adam Lincoln, Sam Robbins and senior helmsman Ady Woods on board. (Paul Russell)

D-568 *Seahorse III* on service to the local fishing boat *Impulsive*, which had broken down in deteriorating weather conditions on 1 May 2004. The vessel was beached after being towed in by the inshore lifeboat. (Paul Russell)

D-568 *Seahorse III* is put through her paces with D-436 *Chloe*, which returned to the station in 2006 for use as a capsize training boat. (Paul Russell)

Relief D class inflatable D-509 *John Kennedy* launching on exercise on 25 April 2007, passing the relief Mersey *Royal Shipwright*. The Land Rover was also on temporary duty at the station while the ILB tractor was being serviced. D-509 was on station from 25 April to 29 August 2007, launching on service six times. (Paul Russell)

Ruby and Arthur Reed II

During the 1960s and 1970s, new lifeboat designs were developed to meet the changing demands on the lifeboat service and the need for lifeboats to reach casualties more quickly. Faster lifeboat types were designed for stations where the lifeboat was kept at a mooring, and in the late 1970s a new type was developed for slipway launching to replace the traditional Watson and Barnett lifeboats and, as at Cromer, the larger 48ft 6in Oakley types. Slipway launching requires a hull design which gives protection to the propellers and rudders, while the hull itself has to withstand the stresses of being hauled up a slipway.

The basic lines plan for the hull of the 'fast slipway boat' (FSB) featured a semi-planing hull constructed from steel, with a shallow draught, long straight keel and flared bow above the waterline. Protection for the propellers was given by partial tunnels, substantial bilge keels, and a straight wide keel ending in a hauling shoe for winching the boat back into its house. The wheelhouse had a low profile to fit into existing boathouses, with a flying bridge amidships and a separate cabin aft of the upper steering position.

The design was subsequently given the class name Tyne, in line with the RNLI's policy of using names of rivers for lifeboat classes, and the prototype, ON.1074, toured the country during 1982 to allow coxswains and crews the chance to see the boat first hand. Once the design had been finalised, a building programme was embarked upon and the sixth boat of the class, ON.1097, was allocated to Cromer. A local appeal, headed by Tony Webster, chairman of the Cromer Branch, was organised to raise the necessary money. The appeal got off to a good start when the remainder of the bequest from Mrs Ruby Reed, amounting to just over £100,000, was donated to the fund, and as this was the largest donation to the appeal it was decided to name the boat *Ruby and Arthur Reed II.*

Ruby and Arthur Reed II was completed during 1985 and arrived at Cromer on 15 December, having been brought from the RNLI Headquarters at Poole. She was formally named at a ceremony on 20 June 1986, being christened by the Duke of Kent, President of the RNLI, with many Cromer townspeople in attendance along with many well-wishers, supporters and holidaymakers. After the service of dedication, the Duke made a speech and then walked down the pier to the lifeboat house and named the lifeboat *Ruby and Arthur Reed II.*

Cromer's first fast lifeboat, the 47ft Tyne *Ruby and Arthur Reed II* on trials. (By courtesy of the RNLI)

The prototype 47ft Fast Slipway Lifeboat ON.1074 visiting Cromer on 1 September 1982 during her trials round Britain. ON.1074 was taken on a tour of the country during 1982 under the command of District Inspector Tom Nutman and Staff Coxswain A. Hunter. While on her way from the Humber to Lowestoft, the new boat visited Cromer, enabling Coxswain Richard Davies, Second Coxswain Billy Davies and Mechanic Donny Abbs, together with former Coxswain Henry 'Shrimp' Davies, to go on board and give the new design their approval. Soon after ON.1074 had ended her tour, the RNLI ordered a further four Tynes from the Fairey Marine boatyard at Cowes, and these were allocated to Padstow, Holyhead, The Mumbles and Cromer. The prototype boat was named *City of London* and in November 1983 went on station at Selsey. The second prototype, ON.1075, was allocated to the Relief Fleet and named *Sam and Joan Woods*. (Top, by courtesy of Eastern Counties Newspapers Ltd; bottom, Paul Russell)

Before Cromer's new Tyne was ready, *Sam and Joan Woods* (ON.1075) came to the station for launching trials to determine what alterations, if any, would be needed to the boathouse. She arrived from the RNLI Depot at Poole in July 1984, directly after the RNLI's public open days, and is pictured leaving the Depot on 21 July 1984 for Cromer. On board are, left to right, Coxswain Richard Davies, John Lee, Honorary Secretary Jim Smith and RNLI Staff Coxswain Jim Hunter. (Paul Russell)

Sam and Joan Woods (ON.1075) arriving at Cromer from Poole for launching and recovery trials in July 1984. Coxswain Richard Davies was in command during the passage from the south coast, with Jim Smith, Honorary Secretary, and a couple of the crew also on board. The trials proved very successful, and showed that very few alterations were needed to either boathouse or slipway. (By courtesy of Eastern Counties Newspapers Ltd)

47ft Tyne *Sam and Joan Woods* at sea with *Ruby and Arthur Reed*, July 1984. The design of the Tyne class was completely different to that of previous lifeboats operated from Cromer. It had a steel, semi-planing hull and was driven by powerful engines which enabled the boats to reach twice the speed of the displacement-hulled Oakley and Watson motor lifeboats. A top speed of approximately eighteen knots was possible, with power from twin 425hp General Motors 6V-92-TI diesel engines. The two main tanks carried 510 gallons of diesel between them, with a reserve tank of 102 gallons, giving a range at full speed of 238 nautical miles. (By courtesy of Eastern Counties Newspapers Ltd)

(Right) Recovery of 47ft Tyne *Sam and Joan Woods* during slipway trials, July 1984. (Paul Russell)

The first launch of a Tyne class lifeboat at Cromer, as *Sam and Joan Woods* goes down the slipway on 23 July 1984. This lifeboat, the second of the Tynes to be built, served for her entire RNLI career in the Relief Fleet. (Paul Russell)

Relief 46ft 9in Watson lifeboat *Guy and Clare Hunter* launching on 18 June 1985 to mark the Royal Mail's 'Safety at Sea' stamp issue. As part of the day's programme, a series of events was organised which included the Orient Express train coming to Cromer and the naming of *Spirit of Round Table* (D-307). (Paul Russell)

Relief 46ft 9in Watson lifeboat *Guy and Clare Hunter* off the slipway on 18 June 1985. She replaced *Ruby and Arthur Reed*, which left Cromer on 4 September 1984 to go for refit and never returned. After a major overhaul at J. E. Fletcher's Boatyard, Oulton Broad, she was placed on station at St David's in December 1985, and remained at Cromer for more than a year while the station's new lifeboat was being completed. The relief boat performed a number of services during this time. The first took place on 4 April 1985, when she went to the small motor vessel *Klass I*, which was aground on the Middle Haisborough Sands. She had to cross the sands as the vessel was on the north-east side, but stood by until the tide had risen sufficiently for the casualty to float off. On 28 July 1985, she assisted the yacht *Helm Spray III*, which had a problem with her steering gear, and her crew were unsure of their position. She proceeded to the casualty, which was about forty miles north-east of Cromer, and located it at 10pm. A tow was rigged but, as the casualty had no rudder, the lifeboat had to use her drogue on the casualty to keep it on course, so the tow had to proceed at half speed. The passage took more than seven hours, and both vessels arrived off Wells harbour entrance at 6.15pm, where the tow was handed over to the Wells inshore lifeboat. *Guy and Clare Hunter*, built in 1955, was stationed at the Isles of Scilly station of St Mary's for more than twenty-five years until being transferred to the Relief Fleet in 1981. (Paul Russell)

In March 1985, some members of the Cromer crew, including Second Coxswain Billy Davies and Mechanic Donny Abbs, went to Poole for training and used the new Mumbles Tyne *Ethel Anne Measures* as *Ruby and Arthur Reed II* was not available at the time. (Paul Russell)

The new 47ft Tyne *Ruby and Arthur Reed II* arriving at Cromer for the first time on 15 December 1985. The new lifeboat was completed during 1985 and arrived at the station on 15 December, having been brought from the RNLI Headquarters at Poole by Coxswain Davies and his crew via overnight stops at Ramsgate and Lowestoft. Upon the new boat's arrival, *Guy and Clare Hunter* was launched so that the new lifeboat could be recovered for the first time after a few minor adjustments had been made to the boathouse. Two launches and two further rehousing exercises were completed, after which Commander George Cooper, the RNLI's Deputy Chief of Operations, who was supervising the boat's arrival, was satisfied that the boat could become operational. (By courtesy of Eastern Counties Newspapers Ltd)

47ft Tyne *Ruby and Arthur Reed II* with *Guy and Clare Hunter* on 15 December 1985 as the Tyne arrived on station for the first time. Soon after her arrival, *Ruby and Arthur Reed II* was launched and rehoused so that the boat could become operational. (By courtesy of Eastern Counties Newspapers Ltd)

Ruby and Arthur Reed II at sea off Cromer pier (top), and being prepared for recovery on 18 December 1985, three days after she arrived on station. (Paul Russell)

HRH The Duke of Kent, President of the RNLI, addresses the crowd during the naming ceremony of *Ruby and Arthur Reed II* on 20 June 1986. She was christened by the Duke of Kent with many Cromer townspeople in attendance as well as lifeboat supporters and holidaymakers.

Ruby and Arthur Reed II on the slipway outside the boathouse during her naming ceremony, 20 June 1986. During the proceedings, the boat was presented to the RNLI by the donor, Mrs R. M. Reed, and the service of dedication was conducted by the Rt Rev The Lord Bishop of Lynn, the Rt Rev W. S. Llewellyn, MA, assisted by Reverend C. W. J. Searle-Barnes, MA, Vicar of Cromer, and the Rev J. R. Sharp, Minister of Cromer Methodist Church. At the end of the ceremony, the Duke of Kent named the lifeboat but the boat did not launch because of heavy swell at the foot of the slipway (Paul Russell)

The 27ft yacht *Phaedra* is brought into Great Yarmouth by *Ruby and Arthur Reed II* on 29 September 1988 after a nine-hour tow in severe weather. (By courtesy of Eastern Counties Newspapers Ltd)

Yacht Phaedra

In the early hours of 29 September 1988, the husband and wife crew of *Phaedra* got into difficulty in force eight to nine winds and had no idea of their position. The skipper managed to connect a car battery to the VHF radio to contact the coastguard, who obtained a bearing on the transmission.

The casualty was thirty miles north-east of Cromer, and *Ruby and Arthur Reed II* was under way just seven minutes after the coastguard's call. Rig stand-by vessels *Desirade, Stout Truck* and *Vulcan Service* stood by the yacht as she drifted in the severe weather. To reach the yacht, the lifeboat was forced to cut across the sandbanks, taking her into very broken water. Coxswain Richard Davies reported later that the lifeboat 'handled well' in the atrocious conditions with 20ft to 25ft waves coming aboard.

At 2.30am the yacht was found, going round in circles with all sails set. At the coxswain's request, the crew lowered the sails and a tow was successfully passed across. The extreme weather and height of the waves made it impossible for a lifeboat crew member to go aboard *Phaedra*, or for those on the casualty to be taken off. In the conditions, Coxswain Davies decided the only possible course was southerly, towards Bacton. In the heavy seas, the tow was very slow with the lifeboat managing only a knot or so and the casualty making very heavy weather. Towing began at 3am and for seven hours the lifeboat crew battled slowly south through the gale until at 10am they reached the lee of the land and conditions improved.

A crew member was then put aboard *Phaedra* and the speed of the tow was increased. After a further two-and-a-half hours at increased speed, the lifeboat and casualty finally reached Great Yarmouth, where the yacht was berthed at 12.30pm. The conditions prevented the lifeboat from being recovered safely at Cromer, so she stayed at Great Yarmouth while the crew returned to the station by road. The lifeboat was unable to return to station for a couple of days because of the severe weather. For this exceptional and difficult service, the Thanks of the Institution on Vellum was accorded to Coxswain Davies.

Ruby and Arthur Reed II launches for lifeboat day, August 1991. (By courtesy of Eastern Counties Newspapers Ltd)

Relief 47ft Tyne *Owen and Anne Aisher* arriving at Cromer for a spell of relief duty in August 1991. She stayed until December 1991 for what was her second stint on station. (Paul Russell)

Ruby and Arthur Reed II is put through her paces on lifeboat day, 6 August 1992, with an RAF Wessex helicopter participating in the air-sea rescue display. Atlantic 21 B-536 from Sheringham was also in attendance. (Paul Russell)

Ruby and Arthur Reed II at Great Yarmouth on 17 October 1993 after the service to the yacht *Happy Bear* four days earlier. (Paul Russell)

Yacht Happy Bear

During the afternoon of 13 October 1993, the 30ft yacht *Happy Bear* got into difficulties in very bad weather. An east-north-easterly force ten onshore wind, gusting to fifty-five knots, was creating seas so rough they reached the lifeboat station doors. As the lifeboat launched, with Coxswain Richard Davies in command, she was completely buried by the seas, frequently disappearing from view as she made her way out to sea, and unable to run at full speed.

Radio contact was established with the yacht at 3.45pm and, using the VHF direction finder, the lifeboat crew located the yacht. They reached the casualty about a mile off Trimingham, and found the skipper hanging on outside with his four-man crew below deck. Coxswain Davies manoeuvred the lifeboat off the casualty's weather beam, and passed across a tow line. The skipper went forward and secured it while another of the yacht's crew took the helm and at 5.07pm the tow began.

The tow proved to be very difficult, and at one point the yacht broached completely, ending up stern-to-stern with the lifeboat, and on another a large sea broke over the yacht, leaving just the skipper's head visible above the water. As they approached land, the skipper expressed his concern about taking his yacht into Great Yarmouth, so Coxswain Davies shortened the tow and went astern, bringing the yacht close enough for Second Coxswain Billy Davies, in complete darkness, to jump across and take the yacht's helm.

Just before 7pm, with only a slight sea, the lifeboat entered Yarmouth and made fast alongside the Town Quay. Due to the severe weather, the lifeboat was unable to return to Cromer until 18 October for rehousing.

For this outstanding service, the Bronze Medal was awarded to Coxswain Davies and in his official report Tim Harrison, the Deputy Inspector of Lifeboats, said: 'The launch was the roughest the station had experienced in the thirty years the coxswain had been involved.'

Lifeboat day 1996: *Ruby and Arthur Reed II* performs a joint exercise with the RAF rescue helicopter for the benefit of holidaymakers ashore. (Paul Russell)

Recovery of *Ruby and Arthur Reed II* after lifeboat day in August 1996, the last to take place from the 1923 lifeboat house. (Paul Russell)

A new lifeboat station

During the 1990s, the lifeboat house and slipway at the end of the pier started showing signs of age and required ever more maintenance work to remain in an operational condition. After more than seventy years of exposure to North Sea storms and gales, the structure was becoming more difficult and costly to repair. Work had been carried out during the 1950s and 1960s, and emergency repairs on the slipway had to be undertaken in the early 1990s, but these were short-term measures.

As a result of a survey of the structure and a review of future requirements for lifeboat cover at Cromer, in 1995 the RNLI decided to replace the entire boathouse and slipway. Cromer was a key lifeboat station, and slipway launching was seen as the most effective method of getting the boat afloat. The next lifeboat to serve the station was larger in every respect than the Tyne, which was already a tight fit in the boathouse. Building a new, larger boathouse, with better facilities, was the only suitable option.

Design studies were undertaken during 1995 by Bondesign Associates and the construction work took place in 1997 and 1998. The exposed conditions at the end of the pier meant that the new lifeboat house had to be built to last. The intention was that it would be used for at least as many years as the building it replaced. Designed for the new Tamar fast slipway lifeboat then on the drawing board, the new house was more than twice the size of the house which it replaced. Incorporated in the building were a tipping platform for the boat, offices, mechanic's workshop, crew room, a changing room, toilets and shower, as well as a souvenir shop and visitor viewing area.

Before work on the new lifeboat house began, the relief 12m Mersey *Her Majesty the Queen* was sent to the station and was launched by tractor and carriage over the beach. The first launching and recovery trials of the Mersey took place in November 1995, and the boat returned a year later for further practice launches before being placed on temporary station duty on 17 November 1996. The last launch by *Ruby and Arthur Reed II* from the 1923 boathouse took place in November 1996 and the Tyne was then taken away. She served in the Relief Fleet until the boathouse and slipway had been completed more than two years later, with the Mersey operating throughout.

The 1923-built boathouse at the end of the pier. The house was much altered internally throughout its life, including modifications in 1984 to accommodate a Tyne class lifeboat, but by the mid-1990s was in need of replacement. (Nicholas Leach)

The historic last launch of *Ruby and Arthur Reed II* from the 1923 lifeboat house at the end of the pier before it was demolished to make way for the new house, November 1996. (Paul Russell)

Ruby and Arthur Reed II leaves Cromer, having launched from the 1923 boathouse for the last time, passes onlookers at the end of the pier, November 1996. (Paul Russell)

Farewell to the 47ft Tyne: *Ruby and Arthur Reed II*, with relief 12m Mersey *Her Majesty The Queen*, after the last launch from the 1923 lifeboat house, November 1996. The Tyne passed the end of the pier after launching, escorted by the 12m Mersey. Also on hand for the occasion was Atlantic 75 *Manchester Unity of Oddfellows* (bottom) from Sheringham. The Tyne was away from the station for almost three years, during which time she served in the Relief Fleet after being refitted at Langney Marine, Eastbourne. (Paul Russell)

12m Mersey *Her Majesty The Queen* is beached on 16 November 1996, during the training period before she went on station. She had arrived on 12 November and became operational after four days of crew training. While the new lifeboat house was being constructed, the all-weather lifeboat was operated from the beach and launched by tractor and carriage. *Her Majesty the Queen* had first gone to the station on 12 November 1995 for a series of launching and recovery trials under the supervision of the Divisional Inspector. She returned a year later and, after further practice launches over the weekend of 16-17 November 1996, was placed on temporary station duty on 17 November 1996. (Paul Russell)

Launch of 12m Mersey *Her Majesty The Queen* with Talus MB-H launching tractor T98 providing the power to push the boat into the water. Launching from the carriage was relatively speedy and the boat's powerful engines easily got her away from the beach and through the surf. The Mersey was launched far more easily and safely than any of the lifeboats of the nineteenth century, which also put to sea from this beach and whose crews and launchers faced the same conditions. The physically demanding and often time-consuming task of actually launching a pulling lifeboat could take many hours. (Paul Russell)

Recovery of 12m Mersey *Her Majesty The Queen*, 16 November 1996, as she is hauled out of the water and then stern-first onto the launching carriage on the East Beach. The complicated recovery procedure was made easier by the powerful Talus MB-H tractor. (Paul Russell)

Relief 12m Mersey *Her Majesty The Queen* on her carriage at the East Gangway, during her period of Temporary Station Duty at Cromer. The 1923 boathouse has been removed, and work on building the new boathouse began in July 1997. (Nicholas Leach)

Against the backdrop of the town and the impressive church spire, *Her Majesty The Queen* is hauled onto her launching carriage during a recovery at low water. (Paul Russell)

Launch of 12m Mersey *Her Majesty The Queen* on exercise on 14 September 1997, with the piling for the new lifeboat house and slipway visible in the background. (Paul Russell)

Her Majesty The Queen sets off from the beach on exercise, 14 September 1997. (Paul Russell)

12m Mersey *Her Majesty The Queen* passes the pier after launching for National Lifeboat Stations Open Day, June 1998. (Nicholas Leach)

12m Mersey *Her Majesty The Queen* launching on service to the yacht *It's Only Me*, 12 August 1998, which had steering failure and a broken rudder. The yacht was towed towards Great Yarmouth until the tow was passed to the Gorleston lifeboat *Samarbeta*. (Paul Russell)

Her Majesty The Queen is recovered following a routine exercise in September 1998, with the new boathouse and slipway in the background nearing completion. (Paul Russell)

The beginning: piling work at the end of the pier during 1997 to provide the foundations and support for the new lifeboat house. The new house, built by May Gurney Construction, was designed by Bondesign Associates and funded from the bequests of Kenneth Brian Shaw, Howard and Margot Backhouse, a gift from Brenda Green, together with donations in memory of Michael Victor Harman and Herbert James Raven. (Paul Russell)

When piling work was complete, the framework and the floor of the boathouse were put in place and the building began to take shape. The new building was much larger than its predecessor, and was intended to accommodate the next generation of fast slipway lifeboat under development during the late 1990s and early years of the twenty-first century. (Paul Russell)

View from the jack-up barge looking at the framework of the new boathouse. The project required careful planning in order for the building to blend in with the character of the pier. The RNLI worked closely with the necessary local authorities and endeavoured to keep local people informed of developments. (Paul Russell)

The lifeboat house and slipway largely complete with finishing touches being applied to the outside of the boathouse. Construction work took place during 1997 and 1998 and proved to be a long and complicated process. (Paul Russell)

The completed lifeboat house and slipway at the end of the pier. Amongst the finishing touches was installation of the hydraulic cradle which tipped the lifeboat into position for launching. Once the winch had been installed, the first slipway trials took place on 17 October 1998, when relief 47ft Tyne *Sam and Joan Woods* successfully completed three launches to become the first lifeboat to use the new boathouse. After several weeks of trials, the boathouse was declared operational on 4 March 1999, which coincided with the 175th anniversary of the RNLI's founding. (Nicholas Leach)

Slipway trials on 4 January 1999 with *Sam and Joan Woods* launching from the new station. She was then slowly hauled back up and onto the tipping cradle. (Paul Russell)

Sam and Joan Woods about to be recovered up the slipway following an exercise launch in January 1999. (Paul Russell)

The first lifeboat to use the new lifeboat house was the relief 47ft Tyne *Sam and Joan Woods*, which had served on relief at Cromer. She is pictured inside the boathouse while the finishing touches are put to the building, 1 November 1998. (Paul Russell)

The opening and dedication ceremony for the new lifeboat house and slipway was held on 20 May 1999. The proceedings were opened by the Cromer Station Branch Chairman, Tony Webster. The keys to the new lifeboat house were then handed over by Alan Koran, Chairman of May Gurney Construction, the company who carried out the work on the new house. The service of dedication was conducted by The Right Reverend Peter Nott, Bishop of Norwich, assisted by Canon David Hayden, Vicar of Cromer and Branch Honorary Chaplain. A plaque in the boathouse was unveiled by the Bishop to mark the occasion. (Paul Russell)

Ruby and Arthur Reed II inside the lifeboat house, June 1999, during the RNLI's 175th anniversary year, which was also the first year of the building's operational life. (Nicholas Leach)

Relief 47ft Tyne *Mariner's Friend* inside the lifeboat house. She served from 12 February to 6 March 2000 while *Ruby and Arthur Reed II* went to Goodchild Marine at Burgh Castle to have a propeller shaft checked following damage sustained on service on 16 December 1999. (Paul Russell)

An unusual photograph showing relief 47ft Tyne *City of Sheffield*, with 'Hartlepool Lifeboat' still on her stern, launching on exercise on 3 December 2000. This lifeboat served at Hartlepool from 1997 to 2000, having originally been built for Whitby in 1988. She came to Cromer on 25 October 2005 from Hartlepool after being replaced there. (Paul Russell)

Relief 47ft Tyne *St Cybi II (Civil Service No.40)* launching on exercise with the Divisional inspector on board. This launch was shown live on the ITV regional news programme *Anglia Tonight* on Wednesday 5 August 2003. Built originally for service at Holyhead, *St Cybi II* was on relief duty at Cromer from 12 July to 9 August 2003, during which time she launched twice on service. (Paul Russell)

Relief 47ft Tyne *Lord Saltoun* on exercise with relief D class inflatable D-465 *Palmer Bayer*, June 2002. The Tyne was on station from 18 February to 10 July 2002, launching five times on service. (Paul Russell)

Relief 47ft Tyne *Sarah Emily Harrop* arriving for relief duties in the early hours of 19 February 2006. She was at Cromer from then until 10 March 2006. Built in 1990, *Sarah Emily Harrop* served at Lytham St Annes for seven years before being placed in the Relief Fleet. She was placed on station at Calshot in February 2007. (Paul Russell)

Ruby and Arthur Reed II on exercise, at sea off the pier with the station's D class inflatable D-436 *Chloe*, and being recovered up the slipway at the end of the exercise, 27 June 1999. (Nicholas Leach)

Wells, Sheringham and Cromer lifeboats together on Sunday 5 September 2004 during a joint exercise off Blakeney. It also involved the relief D class D-446 from Wells. Joining the Tyne lifeboat from Cromer (pictured left) were 12m Mersey *Doris M. Mann of Ampthill* from Wells and Atlantic 75 *Manchester Unity of Oddfellows* from Sheringham. (Paul Russell)

Ruby and Arthur Reed II launching for a routine exercise in May 2006. (Nicholas Leach)

As part of the 200th anniversary celebrations of the Cromer lifeboats in 2004, the restored pulling and sailing lifeboat *Queen Victoria* was launched from the beach on 17 August with a crew of former lifeboatmen from North Norfolk. *Ruby and Arthur Reed II* was also to have taken part, but was called out on a shout late in the afternoon; she did return to a rapturous reception just as darkness started to fall. (Paul Russell)

Ruby and Arthur Reed II with the dive boat *Wreckless*, which had been towed from the Haisborough Sands after suffering engine problems, 18 June 2005. (Paul Russell)

Ruby and Arthur Reed II launched to the yacht *Arosa* on the evening of 7 August 2005, and towed the vessel to Great Yarmouth, where she arrived the following day and is pictured at the Quay bringing the yacht to safety. (Paul Russell)

Lester

In 2005 the RNLI allocated a new 16m Tamar class lifeboat to Cromer. The Tamar was designed to replace the eighteen-knot Tyne class lifeboats, such as *Ruby and Arthur Reed II*, and incorporated a number of features to enable it to be slipway launched. The propellers and rudders were protected by a central keel and small side keels, which supported the boat on the slipway. Green Marine of Lymington, manufactured the hull and deck structure for the Tamar using fibre reinforced plastic and DML fitted out the boat.

The most significant features of the new design were its increased speed, twenty-five knots, and the advanced electronic systems fitted on board intended to make the crew's tasks easier. A new seat design was introduced that reduced loadings on crew members' spines in rough weather. The two control stations were also considerably higher to give better visibility, or 'height of eye', than on a Tyne, which was particularly useful when searching for casualties in the water.

Before the new Tamar could enter service, the lifeboat house and slipway at the end of the pier had to be modified. Although built with the Tamar in mind, the slipway needed reprofiling and various other adjustments were necessary in the house. The work took longer than anticipated, and although the new boat was ready by the late summer, she did not arrive at the station until December 2007 having spent more than a month at Lowestoft during which time crew training had been carried out. During the alterations, a relief 12m Mersey was operated from the East Beach and launched by tractor and carriage. Slipway trials were held with relief Tamar *Peter and Lesley-Jane Nicholson* on 23 October 2007 and the new Tamar, named *Lester*, was placed on station on 6 January 2008.

16m Tamar *Lester* pictured at speed off Lowestoft during crew training, November 2007, with Coxswain John Davies at the helm. The boat was powered by twin 1,015bhp Cat C18 marine diesels, a six-cylinder, eighteen-litre engine which provided good acceleration and fuel economy, and a top speed of twenty-five knots. (Nicholas Leach)

Relief 12m Mersey *Royal Shipwright* arrives at Cromer on 10 March 2007 to undertake a series of launching trials and then to be placed on station duty. (Paul Russell)

Royal Shipwright outside the lifeboat house on the East Beach, 10 March 2007, being prepared for refuelling shortly after she had first arrived at Cromer. (Paul Russell)

On 11 March 2007, *Ruby and Arthur Reed II* was launched for a joint exercise with *Royal Shipwright* and the two vessels were put through their paces off the pier. This proved to be the last exercise by the 47ft Tyne because, a few days later, on the night of 20-21 March, a higher than usual spring tide, combined with a northerly gale and very rough seas, damaged the boathouse doors so badly that they could not be opened, leaving the Tyne stranded. On the morning of 25 March, the stores and kit from *Ruby and Arthur Reed II* were moved over to the Mersey, although the carriage-launched boat had been declared operational on 21 March. (Paul Russell)

Royal Shipwright being launched in rough seas on 18 March 2007 as part of the crew training and familiarisation process. Exercise launches from the pier boathouse are usually restricted in bad weather because of the difficulty in recovery with heavy swell at the foot of the slipway. However, such retrictions do not apply to the beach launch, and so the Mersey went to sea to be put through her paces in the heavy weather. She was then recovered on the East Beach, overlooked by Cromer's famous church. (Nicholas Leach)

Ruby and Arthur Reed II launches for the last time from the slipway at Cromer, 1 April 2007, afer the boathouse doors (left) had been repaired. They were damaged in severe gales in March 2007 and could not be opened (Paul Russell)

Ruby and Arthur Reed II on relief duty at Calshot, having left Cromer. She served there from 4 to 12 April 2007, and was then taken to the RNLI Sport at Poole for use as a training boat and emergency relief. She was subsequently sold out of service to the China Rescue and Salvage Bureau. (Peter Edey)

Royal Shipwright alongside the 30m tug *H. T. Blade*, which caught fire approximately two miles north-east of Cromer on 24 June 2007. A Rescue helicopter from RAF Wattisham and the cargo vessel *RMS Riga* also offered assistance. Three lifeboat crew went aboard and the tug was doused with water by the lifeboat. The tug's three crew were safe and well. Two other tugs, *Grey Salvor* and *Grey Vixen*, later arrived on scene and towed the casualty to Lowestoft with the maritime Incident Response Group teams still on board, and the lifeboat was released to return home.

The new 16m Tamar lifeboat official number 1287 under construction at DML yard in Plymouth. She was funded by Derek Clifton Lethern of Southfields, London, left £1.23m to the RNLI when he died in 1992.

Completed and ready for trials, 16m Tamar *Lester* being lifted into the water for the first time, 26 April 2007. The name was created by using parts of the surnames of the donor, Derek Clifton Lethern, and his friend William Foster.

Lester leaving DML for builder's trials off Plymouth. An innovative systems and information management system (sims) was fitted to the boat which integrated systems such as navigation, communications, engine management and radar, displaying details to the crew on flat screens. (By courtesy of RNLI)

16m Tamar *Lester* in storage at the RNLI Depot, Poole, July 2007, while the slipway and boathouse at Cromer were altered to accommodate her. (Peter Edey)

Crew on 16m Tamar *Lester* at the start of a week of crew training at The Lifeboat College, Poole, 8 October 2007, with the station's former 47ft Tyne *Ruby and Arthur Reed II* in the background. On board are, left to right, Ady Woods, Coxswain John Davies, Ady Barker, Mechanic Paul Watling, Martin Steward and Mearl Brown. (Nicholas Leach)

Before *Lester* could be placed on station, the lifeboat house needed modifying and the 38m slipway reprofiling to fit the Tamar's hull. This was undertaken from the platform rig *Haven Seaway*, which arrived on 4 August 2007 and stayed until 3 October. The boathouse was sufficiently ready by December for *Lester* to be housed inside for the first time. (Paul Russell)

16m Tamar *Lester* arrives at Harwich on 14 October 2007 on passage from Poole. She left Poole on 13 October and called at Portsmouth before continuing to Dover for an overnight stop. The next day, she left Dover and stopped at Harwich, where she was escorted in by both station lifeboats, 17m Severn *Albert Brown* (pictured on left) and the Atlantic 75 *Sure and Steadfast*. (Peter Edey)

16m Tamar *Lester* arrives at Lowestoft on 14 October 2007 after her passage from Poole. She left Poole on 13 October and came via Portsmouth, Dover and Harwich, before going on to Lowestoft, arriving about 4.15pm. As well as the six crew from Cromer, Deputy Divisional Inspector Richard Wynn and Divisional Engineer Peter Barnes were on board for the passage. (Paul Russell)

First launch down the slipway of a 16m Tamar lifeboat, with relief boat *Peter and Lesley-Jane Nicholson* hitting the water during trials on 23 October 2007. This boat arrived at Lowestoft on 17 October and headed south again on 23 October to the RNLI Depot at Poole after the launch trials at Cromer. She then went to Barrow on 29 October, via Newlyn, Kilmore and Douglas for slipway trials at that station. (Peter Edey

16m Tamar *Lester* arrives at Cromer on 9 December 2007 for the first time and is recovered up the slipway. She was stored in the boathouse where she was cleaned up after seven weeks afloat in Lowestoft harbour. This included having her anti-fouling repainted in readiness for final crew training, launching and station acceptance trials in January 2008. She performed her first service on 14 January 2008 when she launched to stand by the car carrier *City of Sunderland* ran aground in the early hours of the morning at the south edge of Happisburgh Sands. (Paul Russell)

16m Tamar *Lester* launching down the slipway at Cromer for the first time, 5 January 2008, and (below) passing the pier at full speed. During the weekend of 5-6 January, four launches were undertaken, with Inspector Richard Wynn on board supervising the crew training. Once the crew were proficient in operating their new craft, *Lester* was placed on station at 3.30pm on 6 January and became the latest Cromer lifeboat. (Nicholas Leach)

Coxswains and crews

Throughout the past century and a half, Cromer's lifeboats have been crewed by men from families the names of which have become synonymous with the station. Probably the best known of all is the Davies family, members of which have been manning the lifeboat probably since the station was established, and who continue to do so. James Davies was the first Davies to be coxswain when he took charge of the pulling lifeboat in 1874. He was succeeded by his son John James Davies, who remained as Coxswain until 1902 and married Ellen Blogg, mother of Henry Blogg who took over as coxswain in 1909 and became the most famous Cromer lifeboatman.

Blogg retired in 1947, and since then the four coxswains have all been from the Davies family. The most recent coxswain, John Davies, was appointed in October 2003 to become the seventh Coxswain Davies, taking over from Billy Davies, who in turn took over from Richard Davies, John's father. His appointment ensures that the link between the Davies family and every official Cromer coxswain since the RNLI took over the station in the 1850s continues into the twenty-first century.

Generations of the Harrison, Allen, Balls, Rook, Stimpson, Mayes, Rix and Lee families have also served in the lifeboats. Their names can often be found in the crew lists, together of course with many Davies. Some of the names may be different today, but the crews continue the work of going to sea to help those in distress.

The crew of *Louisa Heartwell* taken during the early twentieth century. The renowned Henry Blogg, soon to become coxswain, is standing at the back, third from left. The crew are, back row left to right: George Rook, Walter 'Kite' Rix, Henry Blogg, John 'Pokey' Balls, Tom Blyth, Bob 'Young Dinger' Blogg, George 'Cossey' Nockels, George Wakefield, Walter 'Katty' Allen, Bob 'Rumbolt' Balls. Middle row left to right: Tom Kirby, George 'Buckram' Balls, Gilbert 'Leather' Rook, James 'Buttons' Harrison, John Cox, George 'Old Dinger' Blogg. Front row left to right: George 'Bluker' Stimpson, James Harrison, Bob Rix.

James 'Buttons' Harrison, Coxswain of *Louisa Heartwell* from 1902 until 1909, when he was forced to retire due to ill health. The Harrisons were another Cromer family who served on the lifeboats until the 1970s.

Charles Payne 'Charlie' Cox, a lifeboat man for thirty-eight years who received the Bronze medal in 1917, plus Vellums in 1932 and 1933. He was drowned, along with fellow lifeboat man Gilbert Mayes, when their fishing boat *White Heather* capsized in July 1934.

James Harrison (son of Coxswain 'Buttons' Harrison) and Robert Rix in their cork life-jackets. They both drowned in May 1907 when their fishing boat *Boy Dick* capsized. This postcard was produced following the death of the two lifeboatmen, and was taken from a card which was originally produced in 1902 and which appears on the preceding page. (From an old postcard supplied by Paul Russell)

William Thomas 'Captain' Davies (centre) with his stepbrother Henry Blogg (on right). Captain was awarded the Silver medal in 1917 when he was acting Second Coxswain for the *Fernebo* service. During his lfieboat career, he also received two Bronze medals and three Vellums, and served as Assistant Mechanic, Bowman and Second Coxswain. Two of his sons, Henry 'Shrimp' and J. W. 'Jimmy' Davies, became coxswains of the No.1 and No.2 lifeboats in 1947 when Henry Blogg retired.

George 'Buckram' Balls, Second Coxswain to Henry Blogg for twenty-four years, joined the crew in 1885 and served until 1933, earning the Bronze medal and two Vellums. In 1934 he became caretaker of the No.2 lifeboat house, a position he held until his death in 1950. His son, grandson and great grandson all served on the lifeboats.

A photograph taken at a dinner given by the Ex-Servicemen's Social Club and residents of Cromer for the crew of the lifeboat in recognition of their gallant services, and especially following the rescue from the steamer *Georgia* by *H. F. Bailey* on 22 November 1927. The dinner was held at the Newhaven Court Hotel, Norwich Road, Cromer, home of Commander Oliver Locker Lampson, on 29 November 1927.

Front cover of the *Illustrated* from March 1940 featuring Henry Blogg. The RNLI exploited Blogg's fame where possible, and he was involved in making six radio broadcasts during the Second World War, starting with an interview on *In England Now* in November 1939, when he talked about the *Fernebo, Sepoy* and *Mount Ida* services. Another interview followed in October 1941 on *In Town Tonight*, where he talked about the rescue of convoy FS559. These were followed by three further broadcasts in March 1942, the first of which was an interview for the Foreign Service, the second an appeal on behalf of the RNLI, and the third in the series *Democracy Marches* in the North American Service. Then, in August 1942, the services to *Convoy* and *English Trader* were told in the series *Into Battle*.

William 'Doll' Rix, who was awarded a Bronze medal for the *Fernebo* service in 1917, was from a Cromer family of whom many were fishermen and lifeboatmen. In 1925 he became caretaker of the No.1 boathouse, and, in 1933, was awarded a long service vellum from the RNLI for 50 years' service. (By courtesy of Ros Davies)

Coxswain Henry Blogg with Lady Suffield at the naming of the first *H. F. Bailey*, 26 July 1923.

A formal photograph of Henry Blogg wearing the RNLI's then standard-issue kapok life jacket.

Henry Blogg with his dog Monte, which was rescued from the steamship *Monte Nevoso* in October 1932.

Robert William 'Skinback' Cox, a member of the crew for many years, whose awards included a Bronze medal and four Vellums. His brother Charles, his son George and his grandson William were also crew.

William Henry 'Pimpo' Davies, one of the sons of Second Coxswain Jack Davies. He was awarded a Bronze medal and four Vellums during his service in the lifeboat. He was tragically killed, along with his wife, children and in-laws, when a bomb fell on and demolished his house in July 1942.

Henry Blogg ready to organise proceedings at the recovery of *Harriot Dixon*, with whistle in hand.

Frank and James William 'Jimmy' Davies, who were drowned on the morning of 5 June 1953, along with fellow lifeboat man Ted Bussey, when their crab boat *Boy Jimmy* capsized close to the beach. Jimmy, who was Coxswain of the No.2 lifeboat at the time, had been awarded three Bronze medals and accorded three Vellums during his lifeboat career. Frank, an assistant mechanic, had also been awarded a Vellum during his service.

Second Coxswain William Richard 'Dick' Davies, Austin 'Stymie' Blyth and Coxswain Henry Thomas 'Shrimp' Davies on board *Henry Blogg*.

Henry William 'Swank' Davies, mechanic from 1933 until 1961, who never missed a shout. He was awarded four Bronze medals and a Vellum, plus a French Lifesaving medal and Humane Society Vellum.

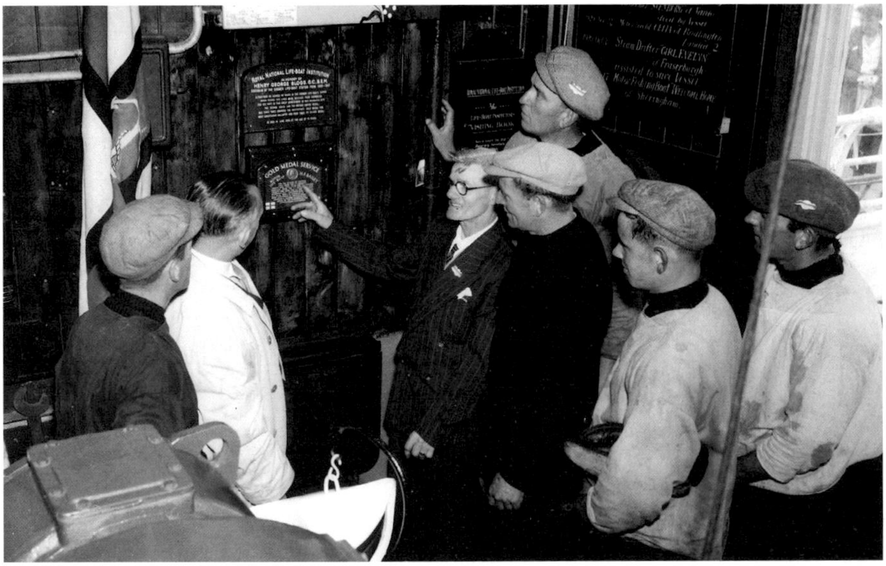

Visitors to the boathouse on lifeboat day, 11 August 1955, included (on left in light coat) Capt van der Hidde and John Smith, with 'Shrimp' Davies and other crew members looking at a plaque that had just been unveiled in memory of Coxswain Henry Blogg. Both men had been rescued by Blogg: Hidde was part of the crew of *Monte Nevoso*, and Smith was rescued from *New Oporto* in 1915.

Members of the Cromer and Wells lifeboat crews during a visit to the Guinness Brewery, 11 January 1966. Wearing their official caps in the middle of the front row are coxswains David Cox and Henry 'Shrimp' Davies. (By courtesy of Donny Abbs)

Members of the No.2 lifeboat visiting Perkins Engines at Peterborough in 1966. Pictured, left to right, are: Richard Davies, Roy Cork, John Blyth, David Leeder, Austin Blyth, Andy Eckett, Donny Abbs, Lewis Harrison, a Perkins employee and Frank Balls. (Photo by courtesy of David Leeder)

The Duke of Kent visited four lifeboat stations in North Norfolk on 4 June 1975. At Cromer he was shown over *Ruby and Arthur Reed*, then visited the Lifeboat Museum and the ILB 'igloo' where he is pictured meeting senior ILB crew members Donny Abbs and Ted Luckin. (Photo by courtesy of Ted Luckin)

Presentation by Coxswain Henry 'Shrimp' Davies to Lewis 'Tuna' Harrison following his retirement in 1975. Pictured left to right are: Jack Davies, Richard Davies, Henry Davies; Jim Smith and Lewis Harrison, 18 October 1975.

TV presenter Pam Rhodes is washed down by, left to right, Clive Rayment, Dick West, Willie Cox and Donny Abbs, after an exercise on the relief boat *William Gammon – Manchester & District XXIX*, 9 March 1979.

Norfolk lifeboatmen past and present at the opening of the new boathouse, 20 May 1999. Standing, left to right: former Coxswain Henry 'Shrimp' Davies, Ralph Amey, Lewis 'Tuner' Harrison, Clive Rayment (obscured), Henry 'Joyful' West (Sheringham), David Cox (Wells), Reg Jonas, Brian Pegg (Sheringham), Jack West (Sheringham), Tony Jordan (Wells) and former mechanic Donny Abbs. Front row kneeling, left to right: Coxswain Richard Davies, John Davies, Gary Humphrey and Billy Davies. (Paul Russell)

Vellum presentation to Second Coxswain Billy Davies for the service to the yacht *Tange* in November 1998. Pictured, left to right, are: Gio Vanzino, Ady Woods, Paul Jeffries, Gary Humphries, Billy Davies, John Balls, John Davies and John Jonas, October 1999. (Paul Russell)

Retirement certificate presentation to crew member John Balls, whose father, Arthur, and grandfather, George, had been long-serving members of the crew. With him are his nephew John (on left) and great nephew John, October 1999. (Paul Russell)

Some of the crew and shore helpers following the service to the yacht *Suli Suli* on the morning of 27 June 2004, following the 200th anniversary ball. Left to right: Richard 'Nelson' Kirk, Ady Barker, John Davies, Richard Leeds, Ady Woods and Sam Robbins. (Paul Russell)

John Davies (Coxswain sinne 2003) with his father Richard (Coxswain 1976-99), at Caister, 26 July 2005. (Paul Russell)

The lifeboat crew pictured on 25 February 2007, left to right: Will Amey, Richard Annis, Ted Brown, Chris Gill, Mike Wass, Craig Davies, Mearl Brown, Seb Gasse, Gordon Nichols, Ady Barker, Alistair Lennox, John Davies, Paul Jeffries, Ady Woods, Charlie Jonas, Paul Watling, Adam Lincoln, Nick Lowe, Tony Webster, Ian van Battum, Richard Leeds (Lifeboat Operations Manager), Paul Russell, Richard Kirk, Sam Robbins, Craig Rogers, Rob Jackson, David Heir, Colin Begley, Kevin Forden, Iain Chambers, Jason King and Ted Luckin. (By courtesy of David Osbourn)

The crew for the final launch of *Ruby and Arthur Reed II* from Cromer, 1 April 2007. Left to right: Dr Alistair Lennox, ex-Coxswain Richard Davies, Iain Chambers, Nick Lowe, Mearl Brown, Ady Barker and Coxswain John Davies. The boat was taken by the Cromer crew to Harwich, and three days later went to Calshot as relief to the Tyne there. (Paul Russell)

The 46ft Watson motor lifeboat *H. F. Bailey* on the promenade outside the East Gangway lifeboat house before she was moved inside to become the centrepiece of the lifeboat museum. The museum was originally housed in the former No.2 lifeboat house. The last lifeboat to use this building was the 37ft Oakley *William Henry and Mary King*, which left in June 1967. The building was converted for use as a museum by the Cromer Branch with many exhibits relating to the station's history. Several major exhibits have been displayed at the museum, but since 1991 the centrepiece of the Museum has been *H. F. Bailey* (ON.777), on station for only ten years but one of the most famous lifeboats to serve the station because she was used by Coxswain Blogg to perform many of his most famous life-saving feats. (Nicholas Leach)

The 37ft Oakley lifeboat *Valentine Wyndham-Quin* (ON.985) outside the East Gangway lifeboat house where she was displayed from 1989 to 1993. She was then moved to Harwich for display in the old boathouse on the Green, where she remains as the centrepiece of the small museum. Built in 1967, she served at Clacton-on-Sea from 1967 to 1983 and then at Clogher Head until 1988. (Paul Russell)

The Henry Blogg Lifeboat Museum at the East Gangway was built in 2005 and was officially opened on 12 April 2006 by comedian Ronnie Corbett (right). The purpose-built museum provides housing for the famous *H. F Bailey* lifeboat (below), which forms the centrepiece of the displays, as well as numerous artefacts and photos relating to the history of lifeboats and life-saving at Cromer. The top floor is occupied by the Rocket House Cafe. (Nicholas Leach)

(Below) Display of the station's service boards inside the Museum.

Appendix 1: Cromer Lifeboats

Pre-RNLI lifeboats

On station (launches/saved)	ON	Length Breadth	Type Power	Name Donor	Year built Builder	Notes Disposal
1805 – 30 (at least 5/31)	—	25ft	Greathead 10 oars	[Unnamed] Norwich Mariners' Association.	1804 Henry Greathead	Transferred to Wells 1830
1830 – 58 (at least 5/15)	—	31ft	Nth Country 12 oars	[Unnamed] Norfolk Shipwreck Association.	1830 Robson, Shields	Taken over by the RNLI in 1857

RNLI lifeboats

On station (launches/saved)	ON	Length Breadth	Type Power	Name Donor	Year built Builder	Notes Disposal
10.1858 – 8.1868 (6/5)	—	34ft 8ft 3in	Peake SR 12 oars	[Unnamed] RNLI general funds.	1858 Forrestt, Limehouse	Broken up 1868
8.1868 – 9.1884 (9/31)	—	34ft 8ft 9in	Self-righter 10 oars	Benjamin Bond Cabbell Legacy of B. Bond Cabbell, London.	1868 Woolfe, Shadwell	Broken up 5.1885
9.1884 – 9.1902 (12/26)	12	35ft 10ft	Cromer 12 oars	Benjamin Bond Cabbell Legacy of Miss Ann Egdell, Alnwick.	1884 Beeching, Yarmouth	Sold locally 1902
9.1902 – 1923 (115/195)	495	38ft 10ft 9in	Liverpool 12 oars	Louisa Heartwell Legacy of Miss E. Heartwell, London.	1902 Thames Ironworks	No.2 boat 1923–31

No.1 station

On station (launches/saved)	ON	Length Breadth	Type Power	Name Donor	Year built Builder	Notes Disposal
1923 – 1924 (3/12)	670	46ft 6in 12ft 9in	N & S motor Single 80hp	H. F. Bailey Legacy of H. F. Bailey, Brockenhurst.	1923 J. S. White, Cowes	To Gorleston, sold 1952
8.1924 – 12.1935 (67/160)	694	45ft 12ft 6in	Watson (M) Single 80hp	H. F. Bailey Legacy of H. F. Bailey, Brockenhurst.	1924 J. S. White, Cowes	Renamed J. B. Proudfoot, sold 1953
4.12.1928 – 5.1929 (3/5)	714	45ft 6in 12ft 6in	Watson (M) Twin 40hp	H. F. Bailey II Legacy of H. F. Bailey, Brockenhurst.	1928 S. E. Saunders	To Selsey, destroyed by fire 1937
12.1935 – 12.1945 (154/448)	777	46ft 12ft 9in	Watson (M) Twin 40hp	H. F. Bailey Legacy of H. F. Bailey, Brockenhurst.	1935 Groves & Guttridge	To Helvick Head, sold June 1973
12.1945 – 4.1966 (99/149)	840	46ft 12ft 9in	Watson (M) Twin 40hp	Henry Blogg RNLI Funds.	1945 Sussex SB Co	To Relief Fleet, sold April 1977

Current station

On station (launches/saved)	ON	Length Breadth	Type Power	Name Donor	Year built Builder	Notes Disposal
30.4.1967 – 9.1984 (125/58)	990	48ft 6in 14ft	Oakley Twin 110hp	Ruby and Arthur Reed Gift of Mrs R. M. Reed, Eastbourne.	1966 William Osborne	To St David's, sold September 1988
16.12.1985 – 17.11.1996 (75/29)	1097	47ft 15ft	Tyne Twin 485hp	Ruby and Arthur Reed II Bequest of Mrs R. M. Reed, plus local appeal, gifts and legacies.	1985 Fairey Marine	Served as Relief lifeboat 1996–99
11.1996 – 24.4.1999 (19/6)	1189	38ft 12ft 6in	Mersey Twin 285hp	Her Majesty The Queen Appeal to Police Constabularies in UK with other gifts and legacies.	1993 Green Marine/ Souter Shipyard	Relief lifeboat on temporary duty
4.1999 – 3.2007 (45/9)	1097	47ft 15ft	Tyne Twin 485hp	Ruby and Arthur Reed II As above.	1985 Fairey Marine	Sold 2008
3.2007 – 1.2008 (9/0)	1162	38ft 12ft 6in	Mersey Twin 285hp	Royal Shipwright Worshipful Company of Shipwrights.	1990 FBM Ltd, Cowes	Relief lifeboat on temporary duty
6.1.2008 –	1287	16m 5.5m	Tamar Twin 1,015hp	Lester Bequest of Derek Clifton Lethern.	2007 Green Marine/DML	

No.2 station

On station (launches/saved)	ON	Length Breadth	Type Power	Name Donor	Year built Builder	Notes Disposal
1923 – 5.1931 (115/195)	495	38ft 10ft 9in	Liverpool 14 oars	Louisa Heartwell Legacy of Miss E. Heartwell, London.	1902 Thames Ironworks	Sold May 1931
1931 – 1934 (3/0)	514	35ft 10ft	Liverpool 12/14 oars	Alexandra Freemasons of London.	1903 Thames Ironworks	Served at Hope Cove, sold 1934
8.1934 – 6.1964 (55/20)	770	35ft 6in 10ft 3in	Liverpool Single 35hp	Harriot Dixon Legacy of Mr W. E. Dixon.	1934 Groves & Guttridge	Sold December 1964
6.1964 – 6.1967 (12/1)	980	37ft 11ft 6in	Oakley Twin 52hp	William Henry and Mary King Legacy of Miss J. G. King, Surrey.	1967 J. S. White, Cowes	To Bridlington 1967, scrapped 1991

Inshore lifeboats

On station (record)	ON	Name Donor	Year built Type
3.1967 – 70 (19/4)	D-101	— —	15'3" RFD PB16
1970 – 10.71 (16/6)	D-26	— —	15'3" RFD PB16
3.1972 – 84 (108/48)	D-197	— Gravesend Branch.	15'3" RFD PB16
1984 – 8.92 (81/30)	D-307	Spirit of Round Table Sheringham and Cromer Round Table.	1984 15'3" RFD PB16
12.8.1992 – 6.2001 (54/6)	D-436	Chloe Gift in memory of Chloe Long.	1992 16'3" Avon EA16
20.6.2001 –	D-568	Seahorse III The Seahorse Ball.	2001 16'3" Avon EA16

Relief lifeboats on temporary duty

On station	ON	Name	Type	Launches/ lives saved
October – December 1920	461	Chapman	35ft Liverpool	0/0
1931 & 1932	680	City of Bradford	45ft Watson (M)	1/0
1940 & 1941	694	J. B. Proudfoot	45ft Watson (M)	7/0
April – July 1952	707	Edward Z. Dresden	45ft 6in Watson (M)	0/0
January – March 1957	781	W. R. A. (No.2 station)	35ft 6in Liverpool (M)	0/0
1958 & 1961	728	Cunard	45ft 6in Watson (M)	3/1
June – September 1964	834	Jose Neville (No.2 station)	35ft 6in Liverpool (M)	1/0
June – December 1965	778	Edward and Isabella Irwin	46ft Watson (M)	0/0
June 1973 – March 1974	821	The Good Hope	46ft Watson (M)	10/4
October 1978 – April 1979	849	William Gammon – Manchester & District XXX	46ft 9in Watson (M)	2/1
September 1984 – December 1985	926	Guy and Clare Hunter	46ft 9in Watson (M)	11/34
April – Oct 1987 & 4 – 25 Mar 1999	1075	Sam and Joan Woods	47ft Tyne	1/0
Nov – Dec 1990 & Aug – Dec 1991	1122	Owen and Ann Aisher	47ft Tyne	0/0
February – March 2000	1142	Mariners Friend	47ft Tyne	0/0
October – December 2000	1131	City of Sheffield	47ft Tyne	0/0
February – July 2002	1138	Lord Saltoun	47ft Tyne	5/0
July – August 2003	1095	St Cybi II (Civil Service No.40)	47ft Tyne	2/0
February - March 2006	1155	Sarah Emily Harrop	47ft Tyne	0/0

Appendix 2: Lifeboat-related items in Cromer

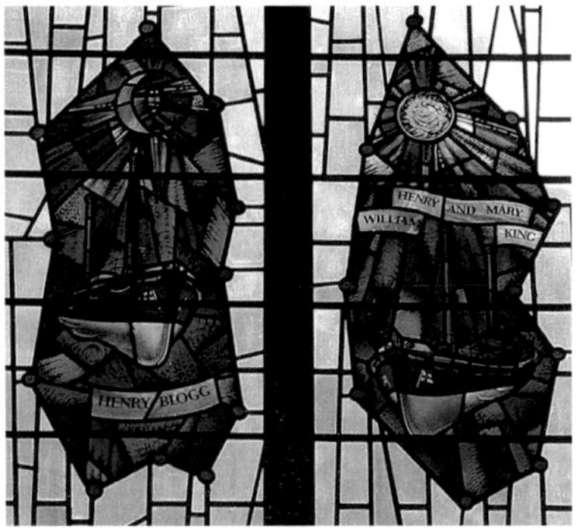

The stained glass windows in the town's church showing the lifeboats *Henry Blogg* and *William Henry and Mary King*.

Henry Blogg Road is one of several roads named after famous lifeboats. The others are Bailey, Dixon and Heartwell.

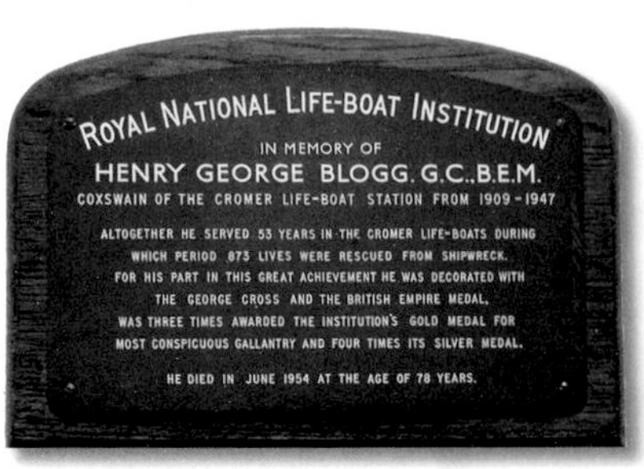

The plaque in the church tower was unveiled on 11 September 1955 by Coxswain Henry 'Shrimp' Davies in memory of Coxswain Henry Blogg. A similar plaque also hangs in the pier boathouse.

The grave of James Davies, who had been Coxswain from 1874 to 1893, shows a sailing lifeboat. It can be seen in the old town graveyard in Holt Road.

The old badge of Cromer High School featuring the lighthouse and lifeboat. Today, the school's 'houses' are named Blogg, Bailey, Dixon and Heartwell.

The mural of Henry Blogg that was hung in The Ship public house in Church Street from 1948; it is now displayed in the town museum.

The bronze bust of Henry Blogg, by sculptor James Woodford, was unveiled by Earl Howe on 23 May 1962 and stands on the East Cliff. The original is displayed in the pier lifeboat house.

The sign on Blogg Cottage, Corner Street, where Henry Blogg lived from 1919 until his death in 1954. During his life it was known as 'Swallow Cottage.'

The compass at the entrance to the pier, pointing towards where the most famous services were performed. The compass design was copied from that on *H. F. Bailey*.